SPECTRUM

Grade

4

CALIFORNIA
Test Practice

Frank Schaffer Publications®

Spectrum is an imprint of Frank Schaffer Publications.

Printed in the United States of America. All rights reserved. Limited Reproduction Permission: Permission to duplicate these materials is limited to the person for whom they are purchased. Reproduction for an entire school or school district is unlawful and strictly prohibited. Frank Schaffer Publications is an imprint of School Specialty Publishing. Copyright © 2004 School Specialty Publishing.

Send all inquiries to:
Frank Schaffer Publications
8720 Orion Place
Columbus, Ohio 43240-2111

California Test Practice—grade 4

ISBN 0-7696-3004-9

6 7 8 9 10 HPS 11 10 09

Table of Contents

What's Inside?

This workbook is designed to help you and your fourth-grader understand what he or she will be expected to know on the California fourth-grade state tests.

Practice Pages

The workbook is divided into a Language Arts section and Mathematics section. Each section has practice activities that have questions similar to those that will appear on the state tests. Students should use a pencil to fill in the correct answers and to complete any writing on these activities.

California Content Standards

Before each practice section is a list of the state standards covered by that section. The shaded "What it means" sections will help to explain any information in the standards that might be unfamiliar.

Mini-Tests and Final Tests

Practice activities are grouped by state standard. When each group is completed, the student can move on to a *Mini-Test* that covers the material presented on those practice activities. After an entire set of standards and accompanying activities are completed, the student should take the *Final Tests*, which incorporate materials from all the practice activities in that section.

Final Test Answer Sheet

The Final Tests have a separate answer sheet that mimics the style of the answer sheet the students will use on the state tests. An answer sheet appears at the end of each Final Test.

How Am I Doing?

The *How Am I Doing?* pages are designed to help students identify areas where they are proficient and areas where they still need more practice. Students can keep track of each of their Mini-Test scores on these pages.

Answer Key

Answers to all the practice activities, mini-tests, and final tests are listed by page number and appear at the end of the book.

Frequently Asked Questions

What is STAR?

STAR stands for **S**tandardized **T**esting **A**nd **R**eporting program. It is the name used for the series of tests given to students in California schools.

What kinds of information does my student have to know to pass the test?

The California Department of Education has created a set of guidelines that list specific skills and information that students must know before moving on to the next grade. Each of these (called content standards, or learning outcomes) is listed in this workbook and clearly explained. Practice activities have been designed to test your fourth-grader's mastery of each California content standard.

Are there special strategies or tips that will help my student do well?

The workbook provides sample questions that have content similar to that on the **STAR** tests. Test-taking tips are offered throughout the book.

How do I know what areas my student needs help in?

A special *How Am I Doing?* section will help you and your fourth-grader evaluate progress. It will pinpoint areas where more work is needed as well as areas where your student excels.

California English-Language Arts
Content Standards

The English-language arts content standards developed by the California State Board of Education are divided into four major sections. The information within those sections tells specifically what your fourth-grader should know or be able to do.

1) Reading
- *1.0:* Word Analysis, Fluency, and Systematic Vocabulary Development
- *2.0:* Reading Comprehension
- *3.0:* Literary Response and Analysis

2) Writing
- *1.0:* Writing Strategies
- *2.0:* Writing Applications (Genres and Their Characteristics)

3)Written and Oral English Language Conventions
- *1.0:* Written and Oral English Language Conventions

4)Listening and Speaking
- *1.0:* Listening and Speaking Strategies
- *2.0:* Speaking Applications (Genres and Their Characteristics)

Language Arts
Table of Contents

Reading Standards

1.0 Word Analysis, Fluency, and Systematic Vocabulary Development

Students understand the basic features of reading. They select letter patterns and know how to translate them into spoken language by using phonics, syllabication, and word parts. They apply this knowledge to achieve fluent oral and silent reading.

Word Recognition

1.1 Read narrative and expository text aloud with grade-appropriate fluency and accuracy and with appropriate pacing, intonation, and expression.

Vocabulary and Concept Development

1.2 Apply knowledge of word origins, derivations, synonyms, antonyms, and idioms to determine the meaning of words and phrases. *(See page 8.)*

1.3 Use knowledge of root words to determine the meaning of unknown words within a passage. *(See page 9.)*

1.4 Know common roots and affixes derived from Greek and Latin and use this knowledge to analyze the meaning of complex words (e.g., *international*). *(See page 10.)*

1.5 Use a thesaurus to determine related words and concepts. *(See page 11.)*

1.6 Distinguish and interpret words with multiple meanings. *(See page 12.)*

What it means:

Vocabulary and Concept Development

- Students should be able to use different strategies to help them determine the meaning of unfamiliar words.
- They should be able to identify synonyms (words that mean the same) and antonyms (words with opposite meanings).
- They should be able to use their knowledge of base words or root words to help them define unfamiliar words. For example, knowing the meaning of the word *reflect* will help them determine the meaning of the words *reflection* and *reflective.*
- They should have a general knowledge of common Greek and Latin terms such as *bios* (life) and *mille* (thousand).
- They should be able to identify the multiple meanings of words. For example, they should know that words such as *act* and *figure* can be used as verbs as well as nouns.

Reading

1.2

Vocabulary

A waiter was taking a break. He said to a brand new employee, "You just have to be the one <u>to break the ice</u> with the chef. Sometimes it seems like he has a <u>chip on his shoulder</u>, but he's okay. This is a busy place. You've jumped <u>out of the frying pan and into the fire</u>, let me tell you. I hope you don't have any <u>pie-in-the-sky</u> ideas about taking things easy here. Some days, I feel like I'm <u>going bananas</u>. It might not be your <u>cup of tea</u>. I think we've got <u>the cream of the crop</u> here; everybody does a great job. It's hard sometimes not to <u>fly off the handle</u> when things are so hectic, though. I think you'll do all right if you don't mind hard work."

DIRECTIONS: Read the passage and then match each idiom with its meaning.

1. _____ to break the ice

2. _____ chip on his shoulder

3. _____ out of the frying pan and into the fire

4. _____ pie-in-the-sky

5. _____ going bananas

6. _____ cup of tea

7. _____ the cream of the crop

8. _____ fly off the handle

A. from a bad situation to a worse one

B. something one enjoys

C. the best available

D. to make a start

E. to lose one's temper

F. seemingly angry or resentful

G. go crazy

H. unrealistic

STOP

Reading

1.3

Reading

Example:

In the word *candle*, *cand* means

- (A) erase
- (B) dark
- (C) glow
- (D) invisible

Answer: (C)

DIRECTIONS: Choose the correct definition for the root in each word.

1. **In the word *abbreviate*, *brev* means**
   - (A) to lengthen
   - (B) to shorten
   - (C) to make a list
   - (D) to learn how to spell

2. **In the word *autograph*, *graph* means**
   - (F) to read
   - (G) to draw a picture
   - (H) to write
   - (J) to measure something

3. **In the word *telescope*, *tele* means**
   - (A) empty space
   - (B) far away
   - (C) close up
   - (D) temperature

4. **In the word *geography*, *geo* means**
   - (F) stars
   - (G) Earth
   - (H) the human body
   - (J) insects

5. **In the word *triangle*, *tri* means**
   - (A) one
   - (B) two
   - (C) three
   - (D) four

6. **In the word *bicycle*, *cycl* means**
   - (F) wheel
   - (G) handlebars
   - (H) spokes
   - (J) chain

7. **In the word *action*, *ac* means**
   - (A) eat
   - (B) fill
   - (C) subtract
   - (D) do

8. **In the word *autobiography*, *auto* means**
   - (F) car
   - (G) friendly
   - (H) self
   - (J) television

STOP

Reading

Word Analysis, Fluency, and
Systematic Vocabulary
Development

Greek and Latin Roots

DIRECTIONS: Read each question. Choose the English word that comes from the Latin or Greek word defined in the question.

1. **Which of these words probably comes from the Greek word *mikros*, meaning *small*?**
   - (A) microscope
   - (B) meter
   - (C) macaroni
   - (D) motor

2. **Which of these words probably comes from the Latin word *centum*, meaning *hundred*?**
   - (F) recent
   - (G) ocean
   - (H) century
   - (J) sent

3. **Which of these words probably comes from the Latin word *circuitus*, meaning *going around*?**
   - (A) curious
   - (B) circuit
   - (C) cirrus
   - (D) cut

4. **Which of these words probably comes from the Greek word *bios*, meaning *life*?**
   - (F) biology
   - (G) bicycle
   - (H) bison
   - (J) binocular

5. **Which of these words probably comes from the Latin word *lampein*, meaning *to shine*?**
   - (A) lampoon
   - (B) lament
   - (C) lamp
   - (D) lamprey

6. **Which of these words probably comes from the Latin word *magnus*, meaning *great*?**
   - (F) magnet
   - (G) mangle
   - (H) major
   - (J) minor

7. **Which of these words probably comes from the Latin word *bene* meaning *good*?**
   - (A) beneath
   - (B) bendable
   - (C) bentwood
   - (D) benefit

8. **Which of these words probably comes from the Latin word *tactus*, meaning *touch*?**
   - (F) tactic
   - (G) contact
   - (H) taco
   - (J) retract

STOP

Reading

1.5

Using a Thesaurus

DIRECTIONS: Use the sample thesaurus to answer questions 1–4.

> **head**, *n.* **1.** skull, scalp, *noggin **2.** leader, commander, director, chief, manager **3.** top, summit, peak **4.** front **5.** toilet, restroom (on a boat) **6.** come to a head, reach the end, or turning point **7.** heads up, watch out, duck, be careful **8.** keep one's head, stay calm, *roll with the punches
>
> **head**, *v.* **1.** lead, command, direct, supervise
>
> **Key:** *adj.* adjective; *adv.* adverb, *n.* noun, *v.* verb. *slang

DIRECTIONS: Choose the best synonym to replace the underlined word in each sentence.

1. **The brain is inside the <u>head</u>.**
   - (A) front
   - (B) top
   - (C) summit
   - (D) skull

2. **Michael asked if he could come aboard our boat and use the <u>head</u>.**
   - (F) summit
   - (G) manager
   - (H) toilet
   - (J) scalp

3. **Captain Blaine was the <u>head</u> of the army.**
   - (A) commander
   - (B) top
   - (C) peak
   - (D) front

4. **"Noggin" and "roll with the punches" are both examples of**
   - (F) verbs
   - (G) nouns
   - (H) slang
   - (J) adjectives

5. **How is the underlined word used in this sentence? She was chosen to <u>head</u> the Art Club.**
   - (A) noun
   - (B) adverb
   - (C) slang
   - (D) verb

6. **What would be another way to say, "Watch out!"?**
   - (F) keep your head
   - (G) come to a head
   - (H) heads up
   - (J) roll with the punches

7. **How is the underlined word used in the sentence? She was able to keep her <u>head</u> when everyone else was panicking.**
   - (F) adjective
   - (G) adverb
   - (H) noun
   - (J) verb

STOP

Reading

1.6

Words with Multiple Meanings

 Clue If you are not sure which answer is correct, eliminate answers you know are wrong and then take your best guess.

DIRECTIONS: Choose one word from the list that correctly completes both sentences.

1. **The player began to _____ .**
   Put the new _____ on the car.
   - (A) run
   - (B) fender
   - (C) weaken
   - (D) tire

2. **The sun _____ at 5:45.**
   A _____ grew beside the steps.
   - (F) appeared
   - (G) rose
   - (H) flower
   - (J) set

3. **My _____ is in the closet.**
   Add a new _____ of paint.
   - (A) hat
   - (B) color
   - (C) shirt
   - (D) coat

4. **Do you feel _____?**
   We get our water from a _____ .
   - (F) well
   - (G) good
   - (H) pipe
   - (J) sick

5. **Mrs. Johnson said Carrie was a _____ student.**
   The light from the headlights was _____.
   - (A) noisy
   - (B) red
   - (C) bright
   - (D) hard working

DIRECTIONS: Choose the answer in which the underlined word is used in the same way.

6. **Please <u>file</u> these papers.**
   - (F) The counselor pulled out her file on the Jones family.
   - (G) Sally used a file to smooth her fingernails.
   - (H) I put the file cards in order.
   - (J) Jane asked her secretary to file the reports on water safety.

7. **I used a <u>lemon</u> to make lemonade.**
   - (A) The color of the baby's room is lemon.
   - (B) That car was a lemon.
   - (C) This cleaner has a lovely lemon scent.
   - (D) Rachel bought a lemon at the store.

Reading

1.0

For pages 8–12

Mini-Test 1

Word Analysis, Fluency
and Vocabulary
Development

DIRECTIONS: Choose the word that means the opposite of the underlined word.

1. The tortoise took a <u>leisurely</u> walk.

- (A) lovely
- (B) swift
- (C) leathery
- (D) delicious

2. She couldn't <u>recall</u> her friend's number.

- (F) forget
- (G) remember
- (H) write
- (J) find

3. Brendan was <u>disappointed</u> when it rained.

- (A) saddened
- (B) pleased
- (C) relieved
- (D) entertained

4. The car was <u>swift</u>.

- (F) shallow
- (G) sluggish
- (H) speedy
- (J) rabbit

DIRECTIONS: Choose the word that best answers the question.

5. José _____ his report to include a section on bugs. Which word means he changed it by adding something?

- (A) wrote
- (B) amended
- (C) erased
- (D) corrected

6. _____, Mom had forgotten the can opener. Which of these words means that it was unlucky?

- (F) Fortunately
- (G) Mournfully
- (H) Excitedly
- (J) Unfortunately

7. Dave _____ around the room. Which of these words means that he walked in a bragging manner?

- (A) tiptoed
- (B) strutted
- (C) ran
- (D) skipped

DIRECTIONS: Read the paragraph. Choose the word that fits best in each numbered blank.

Leslie is becoming _____(8). People know about her art and her athletics. She's _____(9) in the music department for her skills.

8.
- (F) famous
- (G) released
- (H) exhausted
- (J) fragile

9.
- (A) disliked
- (B) prepared
- (C) respected
- (D) always

STOP

Reading Standards

2.0 Reading Comprehension

Students read and understand grade-level-appropriate material. They draw upon a variety of comprehension strategies as needed (e.g., generating and responding to essential questions, making predictions, comparing information from several sources). In addition to their regular school reading, students read one-half million words annually, including a good representation of grade-level-appropriate narrative and expository text (e.g., classic and contemporary literature, magazines, newspapers, online information).

Structural Features of Informational Materials

2.1 Identify structural patterns found in informational text (e.g., compare and contrast, cause and effect, sequential or chronological order, proposition and support) to strengthen comprehension. *(See page 15.)*

Comprehension and Analysis of Grade-Level-Appropriate Text

2.2 Use appropriate strategies when reading for different purposes (e.g., full comprehension, location of information, personal enjoyment). *(See page 16.)*

2.3 Make and confirm predictions about text by using prior knowledge and ideas presented in the text itself, including illustrations, titles, topic sentences, important words, and foreshadowing clues. *(See page 17.)*

2.4 Evaluate new information and hypotheses by testing them against known information and ideas. *(See page 18.)*

2.5 Compare and contrast information on the same topic after reading several passages or articles. *(See page 19.)*

2.6 Distinguish between cause and effect and between fact and opinion in expository text. *(See page 20.)*

2.7 Follow multiple-step instructions in a basic technical manual (e.g., how to use computer commands or video games). *(See page 21.)*

Name _____ Date _____

Identifying Patterns in Text

 Clue Look for key words in the question, then find the same words in the passage. This will help you locate the correct answers.

DIRECTIONS: Read the passage and answer the questions that follow.

> People around the world use energy every day, and some forms of energy are being used up very quickly. But resources like energy from the sun, energy from ocean waves, and hydroelectric power do not get used up completely. These resources last and last. They are called *renewable resources.* *Hydropower* is a renewable resource that is very common. The beginning of this word, *hydro*, refers to water. So hydropower refers to power that comes from water.
>
> What makes hydropower work? A dam, which looks like a tall cement wall built across a body of water, raises the level of water in an area by blocking it. This causes the water to fall over the side of the dam. The falling water pushes against a machine called a *turbine*. The force of the falling water makes the blades inside spin. A machine called a *generator* captures the power from the spinning turbines. This makes electrical energy and sends out electricity to people who need it.

1. Where does hydropower come from?

- (A) sunlight
- (B) water
- (C) electricity
- (D) coal

2. What purpose does the dam serve?

- (F) It blocks the flow of water, raising the level of the water.
- (G) It spins the turbines.
- (H) It captures the power of the spinning turbines.
- (J) It sends the electricity to the people who need it.

3. Resources that last a long time are called _____.

- (A) hydropower
- (B) energy
- (C) fossil fuels
- (D) renewable resources

4. What produces the electrical energy from the water?

- (F) the generator
- (G) the turbine
- (H) the dam
- (J) ocean waves

Name _____ Date _____

Using Reading Strategies

Skim the passage, then read the questions. Refer back to the passage to find the answers. You don't have to reread the passage for each question.

DIRECTIONS: Read the passage and answer the questions that follow.

Clouds

Do you like to watch clouds float by? You may have noticed that there are many different shapes of clouds. Clouds are named for the way they look. Cirrus clouds are thin and high in the sky. Stratus clouds are low and thick. Cumulus clouds are white and puffy.

Do you know how clouds are formed? The air holds water that the warm sun has pulled, or *evaporated*, from Earth. When this water cools in the air, it forms clouds. When a cloud forms low along the ground, it is called fog. Clouds hold water until they become full. Warm clouds that are full of water produce rain; cold clouds that are full of water produce snow. When water falls to Earth as either rain or snow, it is called *precipitation*.

1. **What is the effect of water cooling in the air?**

   (A) Evaporation occurs.

   (B) The sun warms Earth.

   (C) Fog forms.

   (D) Clouds form.

2. **Which sentence explains what causes fog?**

   (F) A cloud forms low to the ground.

   (G) A cloud is white and puffy.

   (H) A cloud is thin and high in the sky.

   (J) A cloud is full.

3. **One effect of evaporation is _____.**

   (A) rain creates moisture in the soil

   (B) the air holds water

   (C) clouds float through the sky

   (D) the sun pulls clouds higher

4. **Write three short sentences that explain how clouds are formed.**

   _____

   _____

   _____

2.3

Making Predictions

DIRECTIONS: Read the passage and answer the questions that follow.

It's as black as ink out here in the pasture, and I'm as tired as an old shoe. But even if I were in my bed, I don't think I'd be sleeping like a baby tonight.

Last summer for my birthday, my parents gave me my dream horse. Her name is Goldie. She is a beautiful palomino. I love to watch her gallop around the pasture. She runs like the wind and looks so carefree. I hope I'll see her run that way again.

Yesterday, after I fed her, I forgot to close the door to the feed shed. She got into the grain and ate like a pig, which is very unhealthy for a horse. The veterinarian said I have to watch her like a hawk tonight to be sure she doesn't get colic. That's a very bad stomachache. Because he also said I should keep her moving, I have walked her around and around the pasture until I feel like we're on a merry-go-round.

Now the sun is finally beginning to peek over the horizon, and Goldie seems content. I think she's going to be as good as new.

1. **What will the narrator most likely do the next time she feeds the horse?**

    Ⓐ She will feed the horse too much.

    Ⓑ She will make sure she closes the feed shed door.

    Ⓒ She will give the horse plenty of water.

    Ⓓ She will leave the feed shed open.

2. **How much experience do you think the narrator has with horses?**

    Ⓕ Lots. She's probably owned many horses before.

    Ⓖ This is probably her first horse. She doesn't have a lot of experience.

    Ⓗ She's probably owned a horse before this, but not many.

    Ⓙ I can't tell from the story.

3. **Based on the passage, which of the following is most likely true about the narrator?**

    Ⓐ She really does not care much about Goldie.

    Ⓑ She is devoted to Goldie and will be dedicated to helping her.

    Ⓒ She will not want to have anything to do with horses in the future.

    Ⓓ The story does not reveal anything about the narrator.

STOP

Reading

2.4

Evaluating Information

DIRECTIONS: Tomas keeps a journal for his All-Year Project in English. On the entry for this day, he wrote about an assignment. Read the journal entry, then answer numbers 1–3.

October 19

"Boy, does this sound like a goofy assignment," I said to Kendra, rolling my eyes. We were walking home after school talking about what Mr. Stewart had given us for homework this week. We were supposed to listen—just listen—for a total of two hours this week. We could do it any time we wanted, in short periods or long, and write down some of the things we heard. We also had to describe where we listened and the time of day.

As we walked by a small corner park, Kendra stopped for a moment and suggested, "Hey, I have an idea. Let's start right here. We should just sit down in the park and get part of the assignment done. It will be a breeze."

I told her it was a great idea, then spotted a bench beside the fountain. "Let's get started," I said.

We sat down and pulled out notebooks and pencils. After just a few seconds, Kendra began writing something down. For the next half hour, we did nothing but sit, listen, and take notes.

At about three o'clock, Kendra said, "That's enough for me now. Do you want to compare notes? I want to be sure I did this right."

"Sure," I answered. "I can't believe all the things I heard. Maybe this isn't such a goofy assignment after all."

1. **Why did Mr. Stewart probably give the students this assignment?**

   (A) It would be an easy way for them to get a good grade.

   (B) It would give them a chance to work together.

   (C) It would give them more free time for other assignments.

   (D) It would help them understand the world around them better.

2. **Tomas and Kendra live in a city. Which of these sounds are they most likely to hear on the way home?**

   (F) birds chirping

   (G) the wind in the trees

   (H) traffic sounds

   (J) planes landing

3. **What lesson did Tomas probably learn?**

   (A) Some assignments are better than they first seem.

   (B) Kendra is a better student than he first thought.

   (C) Mr. Stewart usually gives easy assignments.

   (D) There is no reason to go right home after school.

Reading

2.5

Comparing and Contrasting Information

DIRECTIONS: Read the passages and answer the questions that follow.

Pompeii

Almost 2,000 years ago, Pompeii was a rich and beautiful city in Italy on the Bay of Naples. The city lay close to a great volcano, Mount Vesuvius.

One day, Vesuvius began to rumble and erupt. Lava, steam, and ash burst from the volcano. Soon the sky was black with ash. The ash rained down on Pompeii. The people tried to hide in buildings or escape to the sea in boats. But the ash fell so quickly that people were buried wherever they were. The city was covered with over 12 feet of ash.

Scientists have found the remains of Pompeii. Much of what they have found is just as it was the day Mount Vesuvius erupted. This discovery has helped us learn more about ancient Roman times.

Rabaul

Rabaul is a small town in Papua New Guinea. It is located on a huge volcanic crater. People who live there today know that the volcano has erupted before, so they have made an escape plan. In 1994, there was a major volcanic eruption in Rabaul. Just before the eruption, scientists noticed strong earthquakes. They warned the people to leave, or evacuate. There was very little notice, but people were able to begin their escape plan. On the day of the eruption, earthquakes shook Rabaul. More than 50,000 people left the area. Volcanic ash filled the sky. When the smoke cleared, about three-fourths of the houses on the island had been flattened. The island suffered greatly, but because of planning only a few people lost their lives.

1. **Why were their fewer deaths in Rabaul than in Pompeii when the volcanoes erupted?**

   _____

   _____

2. **Why were the people of Rabaul able to begin their escape before the eruption?**

   _____

   _____

3. **What advice would you give to the people of Pompeii?**

   My advice is if _____

   _____ you run _____

   r _____

   _____

   _____

Name _____ Date _____

Distinguishing Fact and Opinion

DIRECTIONS: Read the passage and answer the questions that follow.

Stonehenge is an ancient monument made up of a group of huge stones. It is located in Wiltshire, England. No one knows who put the stones there or what they are for. Some scientists think that they were put there thousands of years ago by people who worshiped the sun.

Through the years, many of the original stones have fallen or have been carried away and used to build other things. But many stones still stand in place. From these stones and other markings, scientists think they know how the monument looked when it was first built. Some think that Stonehenge was built by ancient people to study the sun. These people may have used the monument to predict changes in the seasons—even eclipses of the sun. Today, Stonehenge is one of the most popular tourist stops in England.

1. **Which of the following is a fact about Stonehenge?**

   Ⓐ Scientists know what Stonehenge looked like when it was first built.

   Ⓑ Stonehenge is located in Wiltshire, England.

   Ⓒ Scientists know why Stonehenge was built.

   Ⓓ Stonehenge helped people study eclipses of the sun.

2. **Which of the following is an opinion about Stonehenge?**

   Ⓕ Some of the stones were carried away.

   Ⓖ Stonehenge is in England.

   Ⓗ The stones are in a circle.

   Ⓙ Stonehenge is the most popular tourist stop in England.

3. **Write *F* if the statement is false and *T* if it is true.**

   _____ Over the years, many stones have fallen or were carried away.

   _____ Only five stones remain as a monument.

   _____ Ancient people may have used the monument to study the sun.

   _____ Stonehenge was built hundreds of years ago.

Following Directions

DIRECTIONS: Read the recipe for strawberry jam and answer the questions that follow.

If you want to enjoy a sweet treat, here is a delicious strawberry jam you can make. You will need:

2 cups strawberries, washed and sliced, with green caps removed (or use frozen ones, without sugar)
1/4 cup frozen pineapple juice concentrate, thawed
1 cup mashed banana (mash ripe banana with a fork)
3 tablespoons cornstarch
3 tablespoons cold water

Mix strawberries and pineapple juice concentrate. Microwave on high for one minute. Stir mashed banana until it is creamy. Mix into strawberries and juice.

Combine cornstarch and water in a small bowl. Add to strawberries. Stir well. Microwave on high for 30 seconds. Stir. Microwave on high for 30 seconds. Stir. Continue until the jam is thick and is dark red. Cool. Store in refrigerator.

1. **Which of these steps comes first in the recipe?**

   Ⓐ Cool the jam and store it in the refrigerator.

   Ⓑ Mix the strawberries and pineapple juice.

   Ⓒ Combine the cornstarch and water.

   Ⓓ Microwave on high for one minute.

2. **After adding the cornstarch and water to the strawberries, you _____.**

   Ⓕ repeat the cooking and stirring until the jam is thick and dark

   Ⓖ freeze the jam

   Ⓗ mash the bananas while the jam is cooking

   Ⓙ add sugar until it tastes good

3. **Which step comes immediately after you mix the banana into the strawberries and juice?**

   Ⓐ Cool the jam and store it in the refrigerator.

   Ⓑ Microwave for one minute.

   Ⓒ Microwave for 30 seconds.

   Ⓓ Combine cornstarch and water.

4. **How much pineapple juice concentrate does the recipe call for?**

   Ⓕ $\frac{1}{4}$ tablespoon

   Ⓖ $\frac{1}{4}$ cup

   Ⓗ 1 cup

   Ⓙ 2 cups

STOP

Reading

2.0

For pages 15–21

Mini-Test 2

DIRECTIONS: Read the passage and answer the questions that follow.

Hibernation

Have you ever wondered why some animals hibernate? Hibernation is when animals sleep through the winter. Animals get their warmth and energy from food. Some animals cannot find enough food in the winter. They must eat large amounts of food in the fall. Their bodies store this food as fat. Then in winter, they hibernate. Their bodies live on the stored fat. Since their bodies need much less food during hibernation, they can stay alive without eating new food during the winter. Some animals that hibernate are bats, chipmunks, bears, snakes, and turtles.

1. The best title for this passage is _____.

    Ⓐ Sleepy Snakes

    Ⓑ The Long Sleep

    Ⓒ Winter Wonders

    Ⓓ Bears and Their Habitats

2. Which of the following statements is **not** true?

    Ⓕ Animals get their warmth and energy from food.

    Ⓖ Some animals cannot find enough food in the winter.

    Ⓗ Animals hibernate because they are lazy.

    Ⓙ Animals need less food while they are hibernating.

3. The main idea of this passage can best be summarized by which sentence?

    Ⓐ Hibernation is necessary for all animals in the winter.

    Ⓑ Hibernation is a time for bats, chipmunks, bears, snakes, and turtles to gather food.

    Ⓒ Hibernation is a long sleep that helps animals stay alive during winter.

    Ⓓ Hibernation means to store food as fat.

Reading Standards

3.0 Literary Response and Analysis

Students read and respond to a wide variety of significant works of children's literature. They distinguish between the structural features of the text and the literary terms or elements (e.g., theme, plot, setting, characters).

Structural Features of Literature

3.1 Describe the structural differences of various imaginative forms of literature, including fantasies, fables, myths, legends, and fairy tales. *(See pages 24.)*

Narrative Analysis of Grade-Level-Appropriate Text

3.2 Identify the main events of the plot, their causes, and the influence of each event on future actions. *(See pages 25.)*

3.3 Use knowledge of the situation and setting and of a character's traits and motivations to determine the causes for that character's actions. *(See pages 26.)*

3.4 Compare and contrast tales from different cultures by tracing the exploits of one character type and develop theories to account for similar tales in diverse cultures (e.g., trickster tales). *(See pages 27.)*

What it means:

Students should be able to compare literary works from different cultures and identify similarities in structure, purpose, and character traits. For example, in some Native American tales, the wolf is often portrayed as a trickster. He plays tricks on other characters to get his way. That same character type is often found in Aesop's fables, as well as in literary works of other cultures.

3.5 Define figurative language (e.g., simile, metaphor, hyperbole, personification) and identify its use in literary works. *(See pages 28.)*

What it means:

Figurative language is language used for descriptive effect. It describes or implies meaning, rather than directly stating it. Examples of figurative language include:

similes - using like or as to compare things that may seem unlike each other; Example: Her smile was as dazzling as the sun.

metaphors - comparing unlike things but without using like or as; Example: His body was a well-oiled machine.

hyperbole - using exaggeration to convey strong emotion, express humor, or emphasize a point; Example: I felt like we walked a million miles!

personification - assigning human qualities, feelings, or actions to an animal, an object, or an idea; Example: The mother bear cried for her cub.

Reading
3.1

Different Forms of Literature

DIRECTIONS: Read the passage and answer the questions that follow.

Fox and the Grapes

One warm summer day, a fox was walking along when he noticed a bunch of grapes on a vine above him. Cool, juicy grapes would taste so good. The more he thought about it, the more the fox wanted those grapes. He tried standing on his tiptoes. He tried jumping high in the air. He tried getting a running start before he jumped. But no matter what he tried, the fox could not reach the grapes. As he angrily walked away, the fox muttered, "They were probably sour anyway!"

Moral: A person (or fox) sometimes pretends that he does not want something that he or she cannot have.

1. **This passage is which genre (type) of literature?**

   (A) poetry

   (B) biography

   (C) nonfiction

   (D) fable

2. **What clues in the story helped you decide what genre it is?**

   _____

   _____

   _____

   _____

   _____

3. **Using the passage as an example, write a definition of this genre. Use the sentences below as a guide.**

   _____ is usually about

   _____

   _____

   _____ includes

   _____

   _____

   _____

STOP

Reading

3.2

Identifying Main Events

DIRECTIONS: Read the passage and answer the questions that follow.

From *The Adventures of Tom Sawyer* by Mark Twain

Saturday morning was come, and all the summer world was bright and fresh, and brimming with life. There was a song in every heart . . . there was cheer in every face and a spring in every step.

Tom appeared on the sidewalk with a bucket of whitewash and a longhandled brush. He surveyed the fence, and all gladness left him and a deep sadness settled down on his spirit. Thirty yards of board fence nine feet high. Life to him seemed hollow, and existence but a burden. Sighing, he dipped his brush and passed it along the topmost plank; repeated the operation; did it again; compared the small streak with the far-reaching continent of fence, and sat down on a tree-box discouraged.

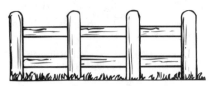

1. **What is the main *conflict*, or problem, in the story?**

   Ⓐ Tom did not know how to sing.

   Ⓑ Tom needed another bucket.

   Ⓒ Tom's brush was not long enough.

   Ⓓ Tom did not want to paint the fence.

2. **What might Tom decide to do next?**

   Ⓕ Spend all day painting the fence.

   Ⓖ Try to get someone else to paint the fence.

   Ⓗ Ask for more instructions on painting the fence.

   Ⓙ Spread paper to keep the paint from dripping.

3. **In the story, the mood changes from _____ to _____ as the plot unfolds.**

   Ⓐ cheerful to sad

   Ⓑ cheerful to glad

   Ⓒ sad to hollow

   Ⓓ sad to cheerful

4. **What would be a good title for this passage?**

   Ⓕ How to Paint a Fence

   Ⓖ A Great Saturday

   Ⓗ All Work and No Fun

   Ⓙ Painting Is Fun

STOP

Reading

3.3

Analyzing Characters

Waterland

"Hurray!" cried Meghan. "Today is the day we're going to Waterland!" It was a hot July day, and Meghan's mom was taking her and her new friend Jake.

Just then, Meghan's mom came out of her bedroom. She did not look very happy. "What's the matter, Mom? Are you afraid to get wet?" Meghan teased.

Mrs. Millett told the kids that she wasn't feeling well. She was too tired to drive to the water park.

Meghan and Jake were disappointed. "My mom has chronic fatigue syndrome," Meghan explained. "Her illness makes her really tired. She's still a great mom."

"Thank you, dear," said Mrs. Millett. "I'm too tired to drive, but I have an idea. You can make your own Waterland and I'll rest in the lawn chair."

Meghan and Jake set up three different sprinklers. They dragged the play slide over to the wading pool and aimed the sprinkler on the slide. Meghan and Jake got soaking wet and played all day.

"Thank you for being so understanding," Meghan's mom said. "Now I feel better, but I'm really hot! There's only one cure for that." She stood under the sprinkler with all her clothes on. She was drenched from head to toe.

Meghan laughed and said, "Now you have chronic wet syndrome." Mrs. Millett rewarded her daughter with a big, wet hug.

1. Which sentence best tells the main idea of this story?

(A) Meghan's mom has chronic fatigue syndrome.

(B) Jake and Meghan miss out on Waterland, but they make their own water park and have fun anyway.

(C) Jake and Meghan cannot go to Waterland.

(D) Sprinklers make a great backyard water park.

2. Which of the following happened after the kids dragged the slide over to the pool?

(F) Jake arrived at Meghan's house.

(G) Meghan and Jake set up three sprinklers.

(H) Meghan's mom stood in the sprinkler with her clothes on.

(J) Meghan's mom was too tired to drive.

3. How do you think Mrs. Millett feels about not being able to take the kids to Waterland?

(A) She's glad that she won't have to spend her whole day with kids.

(B) She feels sorry for herself and is glad she got out of it.

(C) She's disappointed that she can't take them.

(D) She's hurt and confused.

4. What is the turning point of this story?

(F) Meghan's mom feels better and gets wet in the sprinkler.

(G) Meghan and Jake can't go to Waterland.

(H) Meghan's mom gives her a wet hug.

(J) Jake arrives at the house early.

Reading

3.4

Comparing Literature

Walks All Over the Sky
Back when the sky was completely dark there was a chief with two sons, a younger son, One Who Walks All Over the Sky, and an older son, Walking About Early. The younger son was sad to see the sky always so dark so he made a mask out of wood and pitch (the Sun) and lit it on fire. Each day he travels across the sky. At night he sleeps below the horizon and when he snores sparks fly for the mask and make the stars. The older brother became jealous. To impress their father he smeared fat and charcoal on his face (the Moon) and makes his own path across the sky.
    –From the *Tsimshian of the Pacific Northwest*

The Porcupine
Once Porcupine and Beaver argued about the seasons. Porcupine wanted five winter months. He held up one hand and showed his five fingers. He said, "Let the winter months be the same in number as the fingers on my hand." Beaver said, "No," and held up his tail, which had many cracks or scratches on it. He said, "Let the winter months be the same in number as the scratches on my tail." They argued more and Porcupine got angry and bit off his thumb. Then, holding up his hand with the four fingers, he said, "There must be only four winter months." Beaver was afraid and gave in. *For this reason, today porcupines have four claws on each foot.*
    –From the *Tahltan: Teit, Journal of American Folk-Lore, xxxii, 226*

Both of these stories are from different cultures. However, they both try to explain something.

1. What is explained in the first story?

    _Th_____

    _____

2. What is explained in the second story?

    _This_____

    _____

3. Who are the two characters in the first story? In the second story?

    _A_____

    _____

4. How is the relationship between the characters in the first story and the characters in the second story alike?

    _one_____

    _____

    _____

STOP

Reading

3.5

Using Figurative Language

Polar Bears
With fur like a snowstorm
And eyes like the night,
Two giant old bears
Sure gave me a fright.

They came up behind me
As quiet as mice,
And tapped on my shoulder.
Their paws were like ice.

As high as a kite,
I jumped in the air,
And turned round to see
Those bears standing there.

"We're sorry we scared you,"
The bears said so cool.
"We just came to ask you
To fill up our pool!"

DIRECTIONS: Fill in the blanks to complete the similes from the poem.

1. paws *like* _____

2. fur *like* _____

3. as high *as* a _____

4. eyes *like* _____

5. as quiet *as* _____

DIRECTIONS: Write your own similes using these words as a guide. Compare two things by using the words *like* or *as*.

6. a lunch *as* _____ *as*
   _____

7. a friend *like* a _____

8. a coat *as* _____ *as*
   _____

9. a winter day *like* a _____
   _____

10. with _____ *like* sunshine

Reading

3.0

For pages 24–28

Mini-Test 3

DIRECTIONS: Read the passage and answer the questions that follow.

A Bumpy Ride

When we first climbed into the car and strapped on our safety belts, I wasn't very nervous. I was sitting right next to my big brother and he had done this many times before. As we started to climb the hill, however, I could feel my heart jump into my throat. "Brian?" I asked nervously. "Is this supposed to be so noisy?" "Sure, Matthew," Brian answered. "It always does that." A minute later we were going so fast down the hill I didn't have time to think. With a twist, a loop, and a bunch of fast turns, everyone on board screamed in delight. No wonder this was one of the most popular rides in the park. By the time the car pulled into the station and we got off the ride, I was ready to do it again!

1. **Which of the following best describes the setting of this story?**

   Ⓐ a car ride to school

   Ⓑ a train ride

   Ⓒ a ride on a roller coaster

   Ⓓ a trip to the grocery store

2. **What might have happened if this story had taken place in a regular car?**

   Ⓕ Brian might have lost his license for careless driving.

   Ⓖ Brian might have started a taxi business.

   Ⓗ Matthew might have wanted to drive with Brian again.

   Ⓙ Matthew might not have been nervous.

3. **At what point in the story did you realize where it was taking place? What words or phrases helped you understand the setting?**

   _____

   _____

   _____

   _____

   _____

   _____

   _____

   _____

   _____

STOP

How Am I Doing?

Mini-Test 1 Page 13 **Number Correct**	**8–9** answers correct	**Great Job!** Move on to the section test on page 31.
	5–7 answers correct	**You're almost there!** But you still need a little practice. Review practice pages 8–12 before moving on to the section test on page 31.
	0–4 answers correct	**Oops!** Time to review what you have learned and try again. Review the practice section on pages 8–12. Then retake the test on page 13. Now move on to the section test on page 31.
Mini-Test 2 Page 22 **Number Correct**	**3** answers correct	**Awesome!** Move on to the section test on page 31.
	2 answers correct	**You're almost there!** But you still need a little practice. Review practice pages 15–21 before moving on to the section test on page 31.
	0–1 answers correct	**Oops!** Time to review what you have learned and try again. Review the practice section on pages 15–21. Then retake the test on page 22. Now move on to the section test on page 31.
Mini-Test 3 Page 29 **Number Correct**	**3** answers correct	**Great Job!** Move on to the section test on page 31.
	2 answers correct	**You're almost there!** But you still need a little practice. Review practice pages 24–28 before moving on to the section test on page 31.
	0–1 answers correct	**Oops!** Time to review what you have learned and try again. Review the practice section on pages 24–28. Then retake the test on page 29. Now move on to the section test on page 31.

Final Reading Test
for pages 8–29

DIRECTIONS: Choose the word that means the opposite of the underlined word.

1. **rough board**
   - (A) large
   - (B) heavy
   - (C) smooth
   - (D) long

2. **docile animal**
   - (F) vicious
   - (G) gentle
   - (H) shy
   - (J) active

3. **hilarious movie**
   - (A) scary
   - (B) long
   - (C) sad
   - (D) confusing

4. **left promptly**
   - (F) late
   - (G) recently
   - (H) quietly
   - (J) slowly

5. **active child**
   - (A) immobile
   - (B) exhausted
   - (C) bored
   - (D) thrilled

DIRECTIONS: Choose the word that means the same, or about the same, as the underlined word.

6. **attend a conference**
   - (F) party
   - (G) game
   - (H) meeting
   - (J) race

7. **mature person**
   - (A) grown-up
   - (B) dying
   - (C) new
   - (D) green

8. **irritated teacher**
   - (F) excited
   - (G) helpful
   - (H) annoyed
   - (J) boring

9. **baggy pants**
   - (A) loose
   - (B) brown
   - (C) too small
   - (D) made of cotton

10. **elated winner**
    - (F) grim
    - (G) joyful
    - (H) outside
    - (J) unpleasant

GO

Name _____ Date _____

DIRECTIONS: Choose the word that is spelled correctly and best completes the sentence.

11. Do you like _____ movies?

- (A) horrorr
- (B) horor
- (C) horror
- (D) horrer

12. Three _____ people lived in the city.

- (F) milion
- (G) millun
- (H) millione
- (J) million

13. The train _____ arrived.

- (A) finaly
- (B) finnaly
- (C) finely
- (D) finally

14. The _____ is narrow here.

- (F) channel
- (G) channle
- (H) chanel
- (J) chanell

15. The test is _____ .

- (A) dificult
- (B) difficult
- (C) diffecult
- (D) difecult

DIRECTIONS: Read the two sentences with blanks. Choose one word from the list that fits best in both sentences.

16. The waiter asked us for our _____.
Put the numbers in_____ from 1 to 10.

- (F) list
- (G) table
- (H) first
- (J) order

17. The surface of the car was _____.
Mr. Abed gave a _____ speech.

- (A) dirty
- (B) shiny
- (C) painted
- (D) dull

18. What _____ will you be on vacation?
I enjoy eating _____ .

- (F) days
- (G) fruit
- (H) weeks
- (J) dates

19. It's not safe to _____ a boat.
This _____ is too heavy to move.

- (A) sink
- (B) stone
- (C) push
- (D) rock

GO

Name _____ Date _____

Brian went zooming to the park to meet his buddies for an afternoon of hoops. It would have been a perfect day, but he had to drag his little brother Pete along.

"Wait for me, Brian," whined Pete.

Brian walked Pete over to a nearby tree, handed him his lunch, and said, "Sit here and eat. Don't move until I come back and get you." Brian ran off to meet his buddies.

As Pete began eating, he heard the pitter patter of rain falling around him. When Pete saw lightning, he ran for shelter. Suddenly, a loud crack of thunder sounded. Looking behind him, Pete saw the top of the tree come crashing down right where he had been sitting. Brian saw it too, from the other side of the park.

"Pete!" Brian screamed as he ran. At the moment the lightning struck, Brian thought, "Pete's not the drag I always thought he was."

20. What is the main conflict in this story?

- (F) Brian has to drag his brother along to the park.
- (G) There is a lightning storm.
- (H) The tree crashes down.
- (J) Brian thinks Pete is hurt.

21. What is Brian going to the park to play?

- (A) baseball
- (B) tennis
- (C) basketball
- (D) soccer

22. Why does Brian realize that Pete is not such a drag?

- (F) They have fun together.
- (G) He didn't have to save him.
- (H) Pete turns out to be a great runner.
- (J) He realizes that he had been taking his little brother for granted.

Snakes

How much do you know about snakes? Read these snake facts and find out.

- A snake skeleton has **numerous** ribs. A large snake may have as many as 400 pairs!
- Most snakes have **poor** eyesight. They **track** other animals by sensing their body heat.
- Snakes can't blink! They sleep with their eyes open.
- Although all snakes have teeth, very few of them—only the **venomous** ones—have fangs.
- Many snakes are very **docile** and unlikely to bite people.
- Pet snakes recognize their owners by smell. They flick their tongues in the air to **detect** smells.
- Snakes have special ways of hearing. Sound vibrations from the earth pass through their bellies to **receptors** in their spines. **Airborne** sounds pass through snakes' lungs to receptors in their skin.

23. What is this passage mainly about?

- (A) keeping snakes as pets
- (B) snakes' body parts
- (C) venomous snakes
- (D) snakes' eyesight

24. In this passage, *poor* means the opposite of _____.

- (F) rich
- (G) good
- (H) happy
- (J) broke

25. *Numerous* means about the same as

_____.

 (A) number

 (B) many

 (C) few

 (D) special

26. What does *track* **mean as it is used in this passage?**

 (F) the rails on which a train moves

 (G) a sport that includes running, jumping, and throwing

 (H) to follow the footprints of

 (J) to find and follow

27. Which word is a synonym for *venomous***?**

 (A) vicious

 (B) sharp

 (C) poisonous

 (D) huge

28. Which word means the opposite of *docile***?**

 (F) vicious

 (G) shy

 (H) gentle

 (J) active

29. Which word means the same as *detect***?**

 (A) enjoy

 (B) arrest

 (C) find

 (D) hide

30. A *receptor* **_____ something.**

 (F) throws

 (G) takes in

 (H) gives

 (J) sees

31. *Airborne* **sounds are**

 (A) carried through the air.

 (B) carried through the earth.

 (C) always made by wind.

 (D) louder than other sounds.

DIRECTIONS: Decide whether each statement is true or false.

32. A large snake may have 800 pairs of ribs.

 (F) true

 (G) false

33. Most snakes have very good eyesight.

 (A) true

 (B) false

34. Everyone is a little afraid of snakes.

 (F) true

 (G) false

35. Only a few kinds of snakes are venomous.

 (A) true

 (B) false

36. Snakes detect sound in their spines and skin.

 (F) true

 (G) false

STOP

Reading Test
Answer Sheet

1 (A) (B) (C) (D)
2 (F) (G) (H) (J)
3 (A) (B) (C) (D)
4 (F) (G) (H) (J)
5 (A) (B) (C) (D)
6 (F) (G) (H) (J)
7 (A) (B) (C) (D)
8 (F) (G) (H) (J)
9 (A) (B) (C) (D)
10 (F) (G) (H) (J)

11 (A) (B) (C) (D)
12 (F) (G) (H) (J)
13 (A) (B) (C) (D)
14 (F) (G) (H) (J)
15 (A) (B) (C) (D)
16 (F) (G) (H) (J)
17 (A) (B) (C) (D)
18 (F) (G) (H) (J)
19 (A) (B) (C) (D)
20 (F) (G) (H) (J)

21 (A) (B) (C) (D)
22 (F) (G) (H) (J)
23 (A) (B) (C) (D)
24 (F) (G) (H) (J)
25 (A) (B) (C) (D)
26 (F) (G) (H) (J)
27 (A) (B) (C) (D)
28 (F) (G) (H) (J)
29 (A) (B) (C) (D)
30 (F) (G) (H) (J)

31 (A) (B) (C) (D)
32 (F) (G)
33 (A) (B)
34 (F) (G)
35 (A) (B)
36 (F) (G)

Writing Standards

1.0 Writing Strategies

Students write clear, coherent sentences and paragraphs that develop a central idea. Their writing shows they consider the audience and purpose. Students progress through the stages of the writing process (e.g., prewriting, drafting, revising, editing successive versions).

Organization and Focus

1.1 Select a focus, an organizational structure, and a point of view based upon purpose, audience, length, and format requirements. *(See page 37.)*

1.2 Create multiple-paragraph compositions:
   a. Provide an introductory paragraph.
   b. Establish and support a central idea with a topic sentence at or near the beginning of the first paragraph.
   c. Include supporting paragraphs with simple facts, details, and explanations.
   d. Conclude with a paragraph that summarizes the points.
   e. Use correct indention. *(See page 38.)*

1.3 Use traditional structures for conveying information (e.g., chronological order, cause and effect, similarity and difference, and posing and answering a question). *(See page 39.)*

Penmanship

1.4 Write fluidly and legibly in cursive or joined italic.

Research and Technology

1.5 Quote or paraphrase information sources, citing them appropriately. *(See page 40.)*

1.6 Locate information in reference texts by using organizational features (e.g., prefaces, appendixes). *(See page 41.)*

1.7 Use various reference materials (e.g., dictionary, thesaurus, card catalog, encyclopedia, online information) as an aid to writing. *(See page 42.)*

1.8 Understand the organization of almanacs, newspapers, and periodicals and how to use those print materials. *(See page 43.)*

1.9 Demonstrate basic keyboarding skills and familiarity with computer terminology (e.g., cursor, software, memory, disk drive, hard drive).

Evaluation and Revision

1.10 Edit and revise selected drafts to improve coherence and progression by adding, deleting, consolidating, and rearranging text. *(See page 44.)*

1.1

The Writing Process

DIRECTIONS: Read the passage and then organize the information by filling in the Venn diagram with names of mammals from the passage.

Mammals
Did you know that you are a *mammal*? Mammals are warm-blooded animals. Most mammals have hair on their bodies.

Many mammals live on land. People, elephants, rabbits, dogs, and cats are all land mammals. Some mammals, like dolphins and whales, live in the water.

The seal, walrus, and otter are mammals that live on land and in the water.

Did you know there is even a mammal that flies? It is the bat.

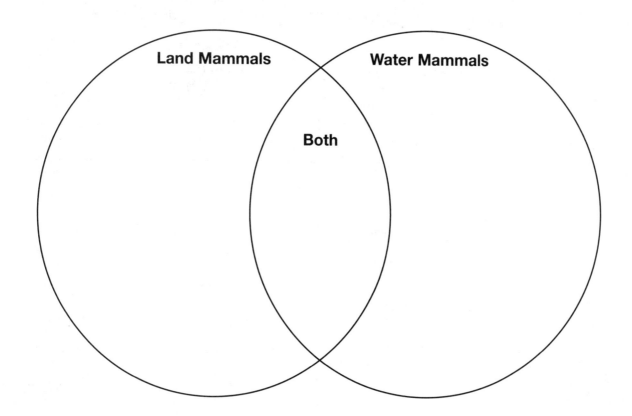

Land Mammals

Water Mammals

Both

STOP

The Writing Process

DIRECTIONS: Read the passage. Then create a summary of the passage by answering the questions that follow.

Glue

Glue is an adhesive. It is used to stick things together. There are three basic kinds of glue: hide glue, bone glue, and fish glue. Glues are made of gelatin, which comes from boiling animal parts and bones.

Long ago, people used other materials as glue. Ancient people used sticky juices from plants and insects. This was mixed with vegetable coloring and used as paint on rocks and caves. Egyptians learned to boil animal hides and bones to make glue. This was much like the glue that is used today.

Today, there are many special kinds of glue. Epoxy glue is made to stick in high temperatures, even if it becomes wet. "Super" glue is the strongest of glues. It can stick even with two tons of pressure against it.

1. What are the three basic kinds of glue?

_____ glue

_____ glue

_____ glue

2. Which is the best definition of glue?

(A) useful for repairs or art activities

(B) an adhesive used to stick things together

(C) something that sticks in high temperatures

(D) mixture of vegetable coloring and bones

3. Complete the summary by adding phrases from the passage.

Glue is used to _____

_____

Glues are made of _____

_____

Long ago, ancient people used

_____ from

_____

and _____

for _____.

Today, there are _____ kinds of glue.

STOP

The Writing Process

DIRECTIONS: Study the outline and answer the questions that follow.

Owls

I. _____

   A. Great Horned Owl

   B. Snowy Owl

   C. Barn Owl

II. **Body Characteristics**

   A. Size

   B. Body Covering

   C. _____

   D. Eyes, Talons, and Beaks

III. **Eating Habits**

   A. Mice

   B. Other Small Rodents

1. **Which of the following fits best in the blank next to I.?**

   (A) Owl Migration

   (B) Owl Habitats

   (C) Types of Owls

   (D) Owl Eating Habits

2. **Which of the following fits best in the blank next to C.?**

   (F) Feather Variations

   (G) Grasses and Leaves

   (H) Trees

   (J) Nocturnal

3. **Explain how the organization of the outline makes it easier to understand the information presented.**

   _____

   _____

   _____

   _____

   _____

   _____

   _____

   _____

   _____

STOP

Writing

1.5

Quoting and Citing Sources

DIRECTIONS: Read the passage and answer the questions that follow.

> **Why Are There Seasons? (from the book *All About Earth*)**
>
> Earth revolves around the sun. It also spins on an invisible axis that runs through its center.
>
> It takes 365 days, or one year, for Earth to revolve once around the sun. Earth does not move in a perfect circle. Its orbit is an ellipse, which is a flattened circle, like an oval. As Earth revolves around the sun in an elliptical shape, it spins on its invisible axis.
>
> Earth's axis of rotation is not straight up and down, it is tilted. This tilt creates the seasons on Earth. No matter where Earth is in its rotation around the sun, its axis is tilted in the same direction and at the same angle. So, as Earth moves, different parts of it are facing the sun and different parts are facing away. The North Pole is tilting toward the sun in June, so the northern half of Earth is enjoying summer. In December, the North Pole is tilted away from the sun, so the northern part of the world experiences winter.
>
> This important relationship between Earth and the sun determines how hot and cold we are, when we plants our crops, and whether we have droughts or floods.

1. **In your own words, describe Earth's different motions in space.**

   _____

   _____

   _____

   _____

2. **If you used information from this article to write a report where would you say the information came from?**

   _____

   _____

   _____

   _____

3. **In words that a kindergarten student could understand, explain how the tilt of Earth's axis creates seasons.**

   _____

   _____

   _____

4. **Where could you find more information about this topic?**

   (A) in an atlas

   (B) in a book of poems about the seasons

   (C) in an encyclopedia entry about seasons

   (D) in an essay about agriculture in the United States and Canada

   STOP

Finding Information

DIRECTIONS: Study the table of contents and answer the questions that follow.

1. **Yoshi wants to find other resources that have information on sunken treasures. In which chapters should she look?**

    (A) Chapters 1, 2, and 3

    (B) Chapters 3, 4, and 5

    (C) Chapters 4, 5, and 6

    (D) Chapters 6, 7, and 8

2. **Which of the following sentences might be found in Chapter 1?**

    (F) The Caribbean is a place many people think of when they hear the words *sunken treasure.*

    (G) One valuable site is *www.yo-ho-matey.com.*

    (H) Treasure ranges from ancient oil lamps to gold and jewels.

    (J) Many treasure ships sank during battles.

3. **Which chapter could help Yoshi identify sunken treasures that no one has claimed or recovered?**

    (A) Chapter 2

    (B) Chapter 3

    (C) Chapter 4

    (D) Chapter 5

4. **Yoshi wonders if there is an area that has more sunken treasure than any other area. Which chapter would be the most helpful?**

    (F) Chapter 3

    (G) Chapter 2

    (H) Chapter 8

    (J) Chapter 4

STOP

Using Reference Materials

DIRECTIONS: Study this entry from an electronic card catalog and answer the questions that follow.

> **AUTHOR:** Lyons, Nick
> **TITLE:** Confessions of a fly-fishing addict/Nick Lyons.
> **PUBLISHER:** New York : Simon & Schuster, c1989
> **DESCRIPT:** 200 p. : 22 cm
> **SUBJECTS:** Fly fishing
> **ADD TITLE:** Confessions of a fly-fishing addict
> **ISBN:** 067168379
> **DYNIX #:** 392312
> Copy Details
> **LIBRARY:** KDL-East Grand Rapids Branch
> **STATUS:** on shelf
> **CALL NUMBER:** 799.12 Lyo : 9/89

1. **Choose the label for the shelf on which you would look for this book.**
   - (A) 500–600
   - (B) 600–700
   - (C) 700–800
   - (D) 800–900

2. **In which section of the library might you go to find more books about fly-fishing?**
   - (F) 500s
   - (G) 600s
   - (H) 700s
   - (J) 800s

3. **What does the *Lyo* in the call number stand for?**
   - (A) the month it was purchased
   - (B) the title
   - (C) the library branch
   - (D) the author's last name

4. **In what year was this book published?**
   - (F) 2000
   - (G) 1989
   - (H) 1799
   - (J) None of these

5. **How many pages are in the book?**
   - (A) 100
   - (B) 22
   - (C) 200
   - (D) 799

6. **At what branch of the library would you find this book?**
   - (F) New York
   - (G) on a shelf
   - (H) 799.12
   - (J) East Grand Rapids Branch

Writing
1.8

Using Reference Materials

Writing
Strategies

DIRECTIONS: Study the sample entry from an almanac's table of contents. Then answer the questions that follow.

Table of Contents

EGYPT

1. In what section would you find the duties of Egypt's president?

   A Government
   B History
   C Population
   D Education

2. Where would you begin reading if you wanted to learn about the people who lived in Egypt long ago?

   F p. 426
   G p. 407
   H p. 428
   J p. 435

3. On what page would you find Egypt's average summer temperature?

   A p. 396
   B p. 402
   C p. 411
   D p. 425

4. Where would you find a list of products that Egypt sells to other countries?

   F Population
   G Imports and Exports
   H Government
   J Coastline

STOP

Editing and Revising

DIRECTIONS: Read the paragraph and answer the questions that follow.

Volcanoes

(1) There are more than 15,000 active volcanoes in the world. (2) Still, know everything there is to know about volcanoes scientists do not. (3) The study of volcanoes is called volcanology, and people who study volcanoes are called volcanologists.

(4) How does a volcano form? (5) Hot liquid rock, called magma, bubbles toward the surface through rock. (6) Once magma has arrived at the earth's surface, it is called lava. (7) Lava builds up until it forms a mountain in the shape of a cone. (8) The spot where lava comes up to the earth's surface through the cone is called a volcano.

(9) Some volcanic eruptions calm, but others destructive. (10) Large pieces of rock can be thrown out of the volcano. (11) People near an erupting volcano can be in great danger from flowing lava and volcanic bombs.

---

1. Sentence 2 is best written

(A) Scientists still don't know everything there is to know about volcanoes.

(B) Scientists don't know everything there is to know about volcanoes still.

(C) Scientists don't still know everything there is to know about volcanoes.

(D) As it is

2. Which of these is not a sentence?

(F) Sentence 8

(G) Sentence 9

(H) Sentence 10

(J) Sentence 11

3. Which sentence could be added after Sentence 10?

(A) Some people collect these rocks after the eruption.

(B) Dust is also thrown out and can cloud the air.

(C) Rocks are also formed

(D) Sometimes the rocks come out with so much force they are called volcanic bombs.

4. In Sentence 11, flowing is best written

(F) flowdering

(G) flowering

(H) flowed

(J) As it is

Writing
1.0

Writing
Strategies

Mini-Test 1

For pages 37–44

DIRECTIONS: Choose the best answer.

1. **What is the name of the part of a book in which references are listed?**
   - (A) bibliography
   - (B) table of contents
   - (C) index
   - (D) glossary

2. **Which would you find in the glossary of a book?**
   - (F) the year the book was published
   - (G) the meanings of words from the book
   - (H) the titles of the book chapters
   - (J) the topics found in the book and where to find them

3. **Which resource would you use to find out when Hanukkah occurs this year?**
   - (A) encyclopedia
   - (B) calendar
   - (C) dictionary
   - (D) atlas

4. **Where would you look to find a word that means the same as another word?**
   - (F) dictionary
   - (G) crossword puzzle
   - (H) encyclopedia
   - (J) thesaurus

5. **Which of the following would probably appear on a map of your state?**
   - (A) locations of gas stations
   - (B) lakes, rivers, and major waterways
   - (C) the street where you live
   - (D) the location of your city hall

6. **In which resource would you look to find the population density of New York City?**
   - (F) dictionary
   - (G) newspaper
   - (H) card catalog
   - (J) atlas

7. **Raina and Miguel have decided to open their own pizza shop. Where should they look to find out how many other pizza shops are in the area?**
   - (A) encyclopedia under business
   - (B) dictionary under pizza
   - (C) Yellow Pages of the phone book
   - (D) atlas

8. **Which word would be a heading for the other words in an outline?**
   - (F) Cans
   - (G) Recycling
   - (H) Glass
   - (J) Paper

STOP

Writing Standards

2.0 Writing Applications (Genres and Their Characteristics)

Students write compositions that describe and explain familiar objects, events, and experiences. Student writing demonstrates a command of standard American English and the drafting, research, and organizational strategies outlined in Writing Standard 1.0.

Using the writing strategies of grade four outlined in Writing Standard 1.0, students:

2.1 Write narratives:

    a. Relate ideas, observations, or recollections of an event or experience.

    b. Provide a context to enable the reader to imagine the world of the event or experience.

    c. Use concrete sensory details.

    d. Provide insight into why the selected event or experience is memorable. *(See page 47.)*

What it means:

Students should be able to write a story about a familiar event. Narratives typically answer the question "What happened?"

2.2 Write responses to literature:

    a. Demonstrate an understanding of the literary work.

    b. Support judgments through references to both the text and prior knowledge. *(See page 48.)*

What it means:

Students should be able to write about the literature that they read. They should be able to use examples from the literature and their own personal experiences to help them support opinions and analyze various literary works.

2.3 Write information reports:

    a. Frame a central question about an issue or situation.

    b. Include facts and details for focus.

    c. Draw from more than one source of information (e.g., speakers, books, newspapers, other media sources). *(See page 49.)*

2.4 Write summaries that contain the main ideas of the reading selection and the most significant details. *(See page 50.)*

Writing Narratives

DIRECTIONS: This is the beginning of a story. Read it and use your own ideas to help you finish the story.

It was finally getting cooler. After a blazing, hot day, the sun had finally gone down. Hannah still couldn't believe their car had broken down. She also couldn't believe her father had decided to walk three miles through the desert for help. The map showed a town up ahead, but they hadn't seen any cars go by for over an hour. She was alone with her mother and her sister, Abigail.

1. What problem does Hannah's family have?

_____

_____

_____

_____

_____

_____

_____

2. Describe two ways that this story might turn out.

_____

_____

_____

_____

_____

_____

_____

3. What are some of the sounds, sights, and feelings that Hannah's family might have experienced?

_____

_____

_____

_____

_____

_____

_____

4. Use the details from your answers to questions 1–3 to write the ending to the story.

_____

_____

_____

_____

_____

_____

_____

STOP

Writing Responses to Literature

The Un-Birthday

In my family we don't celebrate birthdays. At least not like most families. My friends say I have an "un-birthday."

The tradition started with my grandmother. She and grandfather grew up in Poland. They escaped before World War II and made their way to America. When they got here, they were so grateful that they decided to share what they had with others. On their birthdays, they gave each other just one small gift. Then they each bought a gift for someone who needed it more than they did.

As the years passed and the family grew, the tradition continued. On my last birthday, I got a backpack for school. We had a little party with cake and all of that, and then we headed off to the Lionel School for disabled kids. Some of the children are in electric wheelchairs, and only a few can walk. I picked this school because a friend has a sister there.

When we walked in with our arms full of gifts, the kids were really excited. Even though we gave them little things—like sticker books and puzzles—all the presents were wrapped and had bows.

I gave Maggie, my friend's sister, a floppy stuffed animal. Maggie can't talk, but she hugged her stuffed animal and looked at me so I knew she was grateful.

I don't get as much stuff as my friends, but it's okay, even though I want a new skateboard. Seeing Maggie and the others receive their gifts was a lot better than getting a bunch of presents myself.

1. **How do you think the narrator feels about this unusual family tradition?**

_____

_____

_____

2. **How does the narrator know that Maggie liked her gift?**

_____

_____

3. **Why does the narrator call this family tradition an "un-birthday"?**

_____

_____

_____

4. **Would the narrator agree with the saying, "It is better to give than to receive"? Explain your answer.**

_____

_____

_____

Analyzing Information Reports

DIRECTIONS: Read the passage and answer the questions that follow.

> Perhaps you have heard that many types of bats have very small eyes and do not see well. Still, as they swoop through the night, they do not bump into objects and are able to find food, even though they can't see their prey. How is this possible? Echolocation!
>
> You might recognize the beginning of the word *echolocation* as *echo*, and you might recognize the last part of the word as *location*. This gives you clues about how echolocation works. The bat sends out sounds. The sounds bounce off objects and return to the bat. Echolocation not only tells the bat that objects are nearby, it also tells the bat just how far away the objects are.
>
> Bats are not the only creatures that use echolocation, Porpoises and some types of whales and birds use it as well. It is a very effective tool for the animals that use it.

1. **What is the main idea of this passage?**

   _____
   _____
   _____
   _____
   _____
   _____

2. **Why do you think the writer choose to show how the word *echolocation* can be broken into *echo* and *location*?**

   _____
   _____
   _____
   _____
   _____
   _____

3. **What are two questions that you think the writer might answer in later paragraphs?**

   _____
   _____
   _____
   _____

4. **Name some resources that you could use to find the answers to the questions you wrote in Question 3.**

   _____
   _____
   _____
   _____
   _____
   _____
   _____

STOP

Writing Summaries

DIRECTIONS: Read the passage and answer the questions that follow.

The Origins of the Telegraph

Have you ever watched someone tap a key and send a code for S.O.S.? Perhaps you have seen an old film showing a ship about to sink. Perhaps someone was tapping wildly on a device, trying to send for help.

From where did this system of tapping out dashes and dots come? Who invented this electronic device? Samuel Morse invented the telegraph and the electronic alphabet called Morse code.

When Morse was young, he was an artist. People in New York knew his work well and liked it a great deal. Being well known, Morse decided to run for office. He ran for the office of New York mayor and congressman, but he lost these political races.

In 1832, while Morse was sailing back to the United States from Europe, he thought of an electronic telegraph. This would help people communicate across great distances, even from ship to shore. He was anxious to put together his invention as quickly as possible. Interestingly, someone else had also thought of this same idea.

By 1835, he had put together his first telegraph, but it was only experimental. In 1844, he built a telegraph line from Baltimore to Washington, D.C. He later made his telegraph better, and in 1849, was granted a patent by the U.S. government. Within a few years, people communicated across 23,000 miles of telegraph wire.

As a result of Samuel Morse's invention, trains ran more safely. Conductors could warn about dangers or problems across great distances and ask for help. People in business could communicate more easily, which made it easier to sell their goods and services. Morse had changed communication forever.

1. **What is the main idea of this passage?**

   _____

   _____

   _____

2. **Give three details from the passage that helped you answer Question 1.**

   _____

   _____

3. **Use your answers to Questions 1 and 2 to write a brief summary of this passage.**

   _____

   _____

   _____

   _____

   _____

   _____

STOP

Writing

2.0

For pages 47–50

Mini-Test 2

DIRECTIONS: Use the paragraph below to answer the questions.

> **(1)** One of Lucy's friends, Harold, invited her to a special gym. **(2)** This gym has practice walls and safety equipment. **(3)** Lucy enjoys many sports, especially skiing and hiking. **(4)** Harold taught Lucy how to climb safely at the gym. **(5)** When he was sure Lucy was confident, he brought her to Irwin Cliff. **(6)** There Lucy made her first climb. **(7)** Harold is an experienced climber who works as a teacher at the gym.

1. **Choose the best first sentence for this paragraph.**

   (A) I have an older sister named Lucy.

   (B) My sister Lucy is one of my best friends.

   (C) My sister Lucy recently tried a new sport, rock climbing.

   (D) Rock climbing is a sport that is becoming more popular.

2. **Which sentence should be left out of this paragraph?**

   (F) Sentence 1

   (G) Sentence 3

   (H) Sentence 4

   (J) Sentence 5

3. **Where is the best place for sentence 7?**

   (A) Between sentences 1 and 2

   (B) Between sentences 5 and 6

   (C) Before sentence 1

   (D) Where it is now

4. **Which of the following would be most appropriate in a letter asking for information about renting a houseboat on a lake?**

   (F) My sister, my parents, and I are interested in visiting Lake Patterson. Can you send me information about how the lake was created and what kind of fish are in the lake? Are there stores around the lake where we can buy things?

   (G) Last year, some of my friends visited Lake Patterson. This year, my family would like to do the same thing. Can you send me information on how to get to the lake and what to do when we get there? Is it crowded on weekends? What kinds of boats can we rent when we get there?

   (H) My family recently moved here from Minnesota. There are many lakes in Minnesota. We heard that there are many fun things to do at Lake Patterson. Can you please send us information about the lake? What is the weather like in the fall? Do you need a fishing license to fish there?

   (J) My family is thinking about renting a houseboat on Lake Patterson. Please send me any brochures you have that tell how much it will cost and what we should bring. I would also be interested in reading any other information you have on renting a houseboat on the lake.

STOP

How Am I Doing?

Mini-Test 1 Page 45 **Number Correct**	**7–8** answers correct	**Great Job!** Move on to the section test on page 53.
	5–6 answers correct	**You're almost there!** But you still need a little practice. Review practice pages 37–44 before moving on to the section test on page 53.
	0–4 answers correct	**Oops!** Time to review what you have learned and try again. Review the practice section on pages 37–44. Then retake the test on page 45. Now move on to the section test on page 53.
Mini-Test 2 Page 51 **Number Correct**	**4** answers correct	**Awesome!** Move on to the section test on page 53.
	3 answers correct	**You're almost there!** But you still need a little practice. Review practice pages 46–50 before moving on to the section test on page 53.
	0–2 answers correct	**Oops!** Time to review what you have learned and try again. Review the practice section on pages 46–50. Then retake the test on page 51. Now move on to the section test on page 53.

Final Writing Test
for pages 37–51

DIRECTIONS: Choose the best answer.

1. **Ahmed is writing a report on the whales that live in the Indian Ocean. Where should he look for general information about whales?**

    (A) an atlas

    (B) an almanac

    (C) an encyclopedia

    (D) a newspaper

2. **Which of these is the best resource for maps of the Indian Ocean?**

    (F) an atlas

    (G) an almanac

    (H) an encyclopedia

    (J) a newspaper

3. **If Ahmed uses the Internet for his research, which of these Web sites is most likely to give him correct information about whales?**

    (A) a travel agent's site that sells vacation packages to the Indian Ocean

    (B) a government site that gives information about the countries on the Indian Ocean

    (C) a photographer's site that sells pictures of the Indian Ocean

    (D) a school's site that has information from a scientist studying life in the Indian Ocean

4. **Look at these guide words from a dictionary page.**

    pace – packing

    Which of the following could be found on this page?

    (F) package

    (G) pac

    (H) pact

    (J) pad

5. **Look at these guide words from a dictionary page.**

    fourth – fragile

    Which of the following could be found on this page?

    (A) frail

    (B) fourteenth

    (C) fracture

    (D) fountain

6. **If a book's call number is 653.12, on which shelf would you find it at the library?**

    (F) 500–600

    (G) 600–700

    (H) 700–800

    (J) 800–900

GO

7. **In an outline, which of these words would be the best heading for the other words?**

    (A) People

    (B) Government

    (C) Climate

    (D) Bolivia

DIRECTIONS: Read the passage and answer the questions that follow.

Radio

Inventor Guglielmo Marconi came to the United States in 1899. Telegraph communication by wire was already in place, but Marconi wanted to show off his wireless communication—radio.

Marconi's invention could send Morse code without using any wires. He thought this would help with business communication. When introducing his work, he also planned to show how his invention could do things such as broadcasting a sporting event.

Other people had more and different ideas. These ideas led to programs that included spoken words and music being broadcast on the radio. Operas, comedy hours, and important speeches were now being heard in many homes throughout the country. Two famous radio broadcasts were the "War of the Worlds" presentation on October 31, 1938, a fictional story that told about invading aliens; and President Roosevelt's radio announcement of the Japanese attack on Pearl Harbor on December 8, 1941.

In 1922, there were 30 radio stations that sent broadcasts. By 1923, the number had grown to an amazing 556! There was a problem with so many stations broadcasting, however. There was no regular way to do things. Radio station owners organized their stations any way they saw fit.

Even though stations organized into networks, broadcasting still was not organized. The United States government passed laws to regulate radio. This let station owners know which airwaves they could use. The laws also addressed what was okay to say on the radio and what was not appropriate.

Even though television and the Internet are with us today, most homes and cars have radios. It looks as though this kind of communication is here to stay, thanks to Mr. Marconi and his invention.

8. **Which of the following came just before "there were 30 radio stations that sent broadcasts"?**

    (F) There were an amazing 556 radio stations.

    (G) The "War of the Worlds" program was broadcast.

    (H) President Roosevelt announced the attack on Pearl Harbor.

    (J) Guglielmo Marconi came to the United States.

9. **How would you summarize people's reactions to radio?**

    (A) They didn't like it and preferred to watch events.

    (B) It took a long time for them to get used to the idea.

    (C) They immediately liked it and were excited about it.

    (D) They shunned Marconi and thought his invention was too modern.

10. **Which of the following is a fact?**

    (F) Radio was the most helpful invention ever created.

    (G) Mr. Marconi was a genius.

    (H) Radios send signals without wires.

    (J) Radio will never go away.

11. Which of the following is not a supporting detail found in this article?

  (A) The United States government passed laws to regulate radio.

  (B) Marconi won the Nobel Prize in 1909.

  (C) Marconi wanted to introduce his wireless communication.

  (D) Marconi came to the United States in 1899.

12. Why did the author most likely write this article?

  (F) to inform us about the introduction of radio in the United States

  (G) to prove how successful a life Marconi had

  (H) to inspire us to invent more communication devices

  (J) to inform us about all the possible radio shows there are to make

13. Which would be the best title for this article?

  (A) "Guglielmo Marconi"

  (B) "Radio: How Did It Begin?"

  (C) "Radio Is Here to Stay"

  (D) "Wireless, Here We Go!"

DIRECTIONS: Greg is writing a story for the Young Author's column of the school paper.

The first draft of the story needs some editing. Here is the first part of the story.

(1) Our town's name is Lost City. (2) It has an unusual history. (3) First of all, it was founded in 1886 by accident. (4) A group of pioneers thought they were headed toward San Francisco. (5) Instead, they ended up hundreds of miles farther up the coast.

14. Which of these best combines Sentences 1 and 2 into one sentence?

  (F) Lost City has an unusual history and it is our town.

  (G) An unusual history, our town is Lost City.

  (H) Our town, Lost City, has an unusual history.

  (J) With an unusual history, our town is Lost City.

15. Which is the best way to write Sentence 4?

  (A) A group of pioneers toward San Francisco were headed.

  (B) Toward San Francisco a group of pioneers thought they were headed.

  (C) San Francisco, they thought the pioneers were headed.

  (D) Best as it is

Now read the next part of the story.

(1) The founders of Lost City from Baltimore came. (2) They knew about fishing, trapping crabs, and gathering oysters and clams. (3) It was only natural that they would use their skills in the Pacific Ocean. (4) Soon, Lost City was known for its fine seafood. (5) Wagons packed with ice and snow brought fish, oysters, and crabs to inland towns. (6) Seafood restaurants were on almost every corner.

16. Select the best way to write Sentence 1.

  (F) The founders of Lost City came from Baltimore.

  (G) From Baltimore the founders of Lost City came.

  (H) Coming from Baltimore were the founders of Lost City.

  (J) Best as it is

17. Choose the best way to write Sentence 4.

   (A) Lost City was known soon for its fine seafood.

   (B) For its fine seafood, Lost City was known soon.

   (C) Lost City, for its fine seafood, was soon known.

   (D) Best as it is

This is the last part of the story.

   (1) The sleepy little fishing town doubled in size almost overnight. **(2)** Harriet Johnson decided to build a resort on the cliffs near the beach. **(3)** With her fortune, she hired hundreds of workers to complete the job. **(4)** Many of them decided to stay when the job was finished. **(5)** The workers lived in tents on the beach. **(6)** These workers the logging industry that exists even today helped build.

18. Choose the sentence that does not belong in the paragraph.

   (F) Sentence 2

   (G) Sentence 3

   (H) Sentence 4

   (J) Sentence 5

19. Select the best way to write Sentence 6.

   (A) The workers in the logging industry that exists today helped build.

   (B) These workers, they helped build the logging industry. It exists even today.

   (C) These workers helped build the logging industry that exists even today.

   (D) Best as it is

DIRECTIONS: Use the picture of encyclopedias to answer the questions.

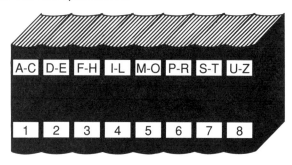

20. Which of the following topics would be found in Volume 5?

   (F) information about the moon

   (G) how to knit

   (H) world climate regions

   (J) the life of Marian Anderson

21. In which volume would you find information about different types of flags?

   (A) Volume 2

   (B) Volume 3

   (C) Volume 5

   (D) Volume 7

STOP

Name _____ Date _____

Writing Test
Answer Sheet

1. (A) (B) (C) (D)
2. (F) (G) (H) (J)
3. (A) (B) (C) (D)
4. (F) (G) (H) (J)
5. (A) (B) (C) (D)
6. (F) (G) (H) (J)
7. (A) (B) (C) (D)
8. (F) (G) (H) (J)
9. (A) (B) (C) (D)
10. (F) (G) (H) (J)

11. (A) (B) (C) (D)
12. (F) (G) (H) (J)
13. (A) (B) (C) (D)
14. (F) (G) (H) (J)
15. (A) (B) (C) (D)
16. (F) (G) (H) (J)
17. (A) (B) (C) (D)
18. (F) (G) (H) (J)
19. (A) (B) (C) (D)
20. (F) (G) (H) (J)
21. (A) (B) (C) (D)

Written and Oral English Language Conventions Standards

Written and Oral English Language Conventions
The standards for written and oral English language conventions have been placed between those for writing and for listening and speaking because these conventions are essential to both sets of skills.

1.0 Written and Oral English Language Conventions
Students write and speak with a command of standard English conventions appropriate to this grade level.

Sentence Structure
1.1 Use simple and compound sentences in writing and speaking. *(See page 60.)*
1.2 Combine short, related sentences with appositives, participial phrases, adjectives, adverbs, and prepositional phrases. *(See page 61.)*

Grammar
1.3 Identify and use regular and irregular verbs, adverbs, prepositions, and coordinating conjunctions in writing and speaking. *(See page 62.)*

Punctuation
1.4 Use parentheses, commas in direct quotations, and apostrophes in the possessive case of nouns and in contractions. *(See page 63.)*
1.5 Use underlining, quotation marks, or italics to identify titles of documents. *(See page 64.)*

Capitalization
1.6 Capitalize names of magazines, newspapers, works of art, musical compositions, organizations, and the first word in quotations when appropriate. *(See page 65.)*

Spelling
1.7 Spell correctly roots, inflections, suffixes and prefixes, and syllable constructions. *(See page 66.)*

Listening and Speaking
[**NOTE:** The California content standards for Listening and Speaking skills are listed here so that you can practice and reinforce them on your own with your student.]

1.0 Listening and Speaking Strategies
Students listen critically and respond appropriately to oral communication. They speak in a manner that guides the listener to understand important ideas by using proper phrasing, pitch, and modulation.

Comprehension
1.1 Ask thoughtful questions and respond to relevant questions with appropriate elaboration in oral settings.
1.2 Summarize major ideas and supporting evidence presented in spoken messages and formal presentations.
1.3 Identify how language usages (e.g., sayings, expressions) reflect regions and cultures.
1.4 Give precise directions and instructions.

Standards (cont.)

Organization and Delivery of Oral Communication

1.5 Present effective introductions and conclusions that guide and inform the listener's understanding of important ideas and evidence.

1.6 Use traditional structures for conveying information (e.g., cause and effect, similarity and difference, and posing and answering a question).

1.7 Emphasize points in ways that help the listener or viewer to follow important ideas and concepts.

1.8 Use details, examples, anecdotes, or experiences to explain or clarify information.

1.9 Use volume, pitch, phrasing, pace, modulation, and gestures appropriately to enhance meaning.

Analysis and Evaluation of Oral Media Communication

1.10 Evaluate the role of the media in focusing attention on events and in forming opinions on issues.

2.0 Speaking Applications (Genres and Their Characteristics)

Students deliver brief recitations and oral presentations about familiar experiences or interests that are organized around a coherent thesis statement. Student speaking demonstrates a command of standard American English and the organizational and delivery strategies outlined in Listening and Speaking Standard 1.0.

Using the speaking strategies of grade four outlined in Listening and Speaking Standard 1.0, students:

2.1 Make narrative presentations:
   a. Relate ideas, observations, or recollections about an event or experience.
   b. Provide a context that enables the listener to imagine the circumstances of the event or experience.
   c. Provide insight into why the selected event or experience is memorable.

2.2 Make informational presentations:
   a. Frame a key question.
   b. Include facts and details that help listeners to focus.
   c. Incorporate more than one source of information (e.g., speakers, books, newspapers, television or radio reports).

2.3 Deliver oral summaries of articles and books that contain the main ideas of the event or article and the most significant details.

2.4 Recite brief poems (i.e., two or three stanzas), soliloquies, or dramatic dialogues, using clear diction, tempo, volume, and phrasing.

Language Conventions

Written and Oral English
Language Conventions

1.1

Sentences

DIRECTIONS: Choose the answer that best combines the underlined sentences.

1. <u>Pedro finished his homework.</u> <u>Pedro went to bed.</u>

   Ⓐ Pedro finished his homework or went to bed.

   Ⓑ Pedro finished his homework then went to bed.

   Ⓒ Pedro finished his homework because he went to bed.

   Ⓓ Going to bed, Pedro finished his homework.

2. <u>The truck brought the furniture to our house.</u> <u>The truck was large.</u>

   Ⓕ The large truck, which brought the furniture to our house.

   Ⓖ The truck was large that brought the furniture to our house.

   Ⓗ The truck brought the furniture to our house, and was large.

   Ⓙ The large truck brought the furniture to our house.

3. <u>Arnie found a ball.</u> <u>The ball was red.</u> <u>He found it on the way to school.</u>

   Ⓐ Finding a red ball, Arnie was on his way to school.

   Ⓑ Arnie found a red ball on the way to school.

   Ⓒ Arnie found a ball on the way to school that was red.

   Ⓓ The red ball that Arnie found on the way to school.

DIRECTIONS: Read each group of words below. Then unscramble them and write them as a sentence beginning with yes, no, or well. Remember to use capitalization and punctuation correctly.

4. **I to you yes will library with go the**

   _____

5. **know no books I about don't monsters any of swamp**

   _____

   _____

6. **sure I'm library's yes the you help will computer**

   _____

   _____

7. **you computer use well do the how library's**

   _____

   _____

8. **well directions start the can by you on computer's following screen the**

   _____

   _____

9. **help you you if yes need the it will librarian**

   _____

   _____

Language Conventions

Written and Oral English
Language Conventions

1.2

Sentences

DIRECTIONS: Choose the answer that best combines the underlined sentences.

1. <u>The tiny squirrel peeked from behind the tree.</u>

   <u>The tiny squirrel scurried away.</u>

   Ⓐ The tiny squirrel peeked and scurried away from behind the tree.

   Ⓑ The tiny squirrel peeked from behind the tree; it scurried away.

   Ⓒ The tiny squirrel peeked from behind the tree and scurried away.

   Ⓓ The tiny squirrel peeked from behind the tree and the tiny squirrel scurried away.

2. <u>Maxine arrived at 6 o'clock.</u>

   <u>Sylvia arrived at 6 o'clock.</u>

   Ⓕ Maxine arrived at 6 o'clock; so did Sylvia.

   Ⓖ Maxine arrived at 6 o'clock and Sylvia arrived at 6 o'clock.

   Ⓗ Maxine arrived at 6 o'clock, as did Sylvia.

   Ⓙ Maxine and Sylvia arrived at 6 o'clock.

3. <u>Janie has a bicycle.</u>

   <u>Her bike is shiny. Her bike is green.</u>

   Ⓐ Janie has a bicycle. It is shiny and green.

   Ⓑ Janie has a shiny green bicycle.

   Ⓒ Janie has a shiny bicycle. Janie has a green bicycle.

   Ⓓ Janie has a bicycle, which is shiny and green.

DIRECTIONS: Choose the complete and correctly written sentence.

4. Ⓕ Having burned dead wood and heavy brush.

   Ⓖ They burn dead wood and heavy brush.

   Ⓗ Dead wood and heavy brush they burn.

   Ⓙ Dead wood will burn heavy brush.

5. Ⓐ The workers in the logging industry that exists today helped build.

   Ⓑ These workers, they helped build the logging industry. It exists even today.

   Ⓒ These workers helped build the logging industry that exists even today.

   Ⓓ These workers the logging industry that exists even today helped build.

6. Ⓕ Helping around the house with cooking and cleaning.

   Ⓖ If the trash basket is full to empty it in the can outside.

   Ⓗ Darren raked up leaves and put them in a large bag.

   Ⓙ The vacuum cleaner heavy to carry up and down and staris.

STOP

1.3

Grammar

 Clue If you are not sure which answer is correct, take your best guess. Eliminate answer choices you know are wrong.

DIRECTIONS: Choose the word or phrase that fits best in the sentence.

1. Carmina _____ left a chocolate bar on the camp table.
   - (A) angry
   - (B) carelessly
   - (C) bravely
   - (D) have

2. The water _____ in the fountain.
   - (F) splash
   - (G) having splashed
   - (H) splashing
   - (J) splashed

3. My mother _____ for three hours.
   - (A) drive
   - (B) driven
   - (C) has drove
   - (D) drove

DIRECTIONS: Choose the line that has a usage error. If there is no error, choose "No mistakes."

4.
   - (F) George Washington
   - (G) are called the father
   - (H) of our country.
   - (J) No mistakes

5.
   - (A) Binoculars are helpful
   - (B) because they let you
   - (C) observe things closely.
   - (D) No mistakes

6.
   - (F) We missed the
   - (G) baseball game however
   - (H) there was a train crossing.
   - (J) No mistakes

7.
   - (A) The junior high
   - (B) play take place on
   - (C) Friday and Saturday night.
   - (D) No mistakes

8.
   - (F) He hasn't never made
   - (G) a mistake on any of
   - (H) his reading assignments.
   - (J) No mistakes

9.
   - (A) We haveta get more
   - (B) decorations for the hall
   - (C) in order to finish.
   - (D) No mistakes

STOP

Language Conventions

Punctuation

DIRECTIONS: Circle the letter of the words that form the contractions.

1. **Tiffany knew she shouldn't go near the deserted old house.**
   - Ⓐ shall not
   - Ⓑ should not
   - Ⓒ will not
   - Ⓓ could not

2. **"Don't even think about going near there," Mom told her.**
   - Ⓕ do not
   - Ⓖ did not
   - Ⓗ does not
   - Ⓙ will not

3. **"There aren't such things as ghosts," Tiffany replied.**
   - Ⓐ were not
   - Ⓑ could not
   - Ⓒ are not
   - Ⓓ cannot

DIRECTIONS: Write the words that form each contraction.

4. **"It doesn't matter," Mom replied.**

   _____

5. **As Tiffany walked past the house one night, she couldn't help noticing the odd sounds coming from it.**

   _____ not _____

6. **The sounds weren't like any other she had ever heard.**

   were not _____

7. **"I mustn't get too close," Tiffany thought as she crept up to the house.**

   _____

8. **"E-E-O-I-O-W," went the sounds. Tiffany didn't move as she saw angry cats race past her.**

   did not _____

DIRECTIONS: Choose the punctuation mark that is needed in the sentence.

9. **Its more fun than scary.**
   - Ⓕ ?
   - Ⓖ !
   - Ⓗ ,
   - Ⓙ None

10. **The puppy couldn't find the food dish**
    - Ⓐ ,
    - Ⓑ .
    - Ⓒ ?
    - Ⓓ None

11. **Max said hed help me rake the leaves.**
    - Ⓕ "
    - Ⓖ ,
    - Ⓗ ?
    - Ⓙ None

STOP

Language Conventions

1.5

Punctuation

DIRECTIONS: Read the passage and answer the questions that follow.

Elizabeth was writing an article for the school newspaper, The Panther's Roar. The story was about wild cats. She decided to base some of her article on the movie The Lion King. She also read an article in a magazine called Animal Antics. The article was titled City Lions. It was about lions that grow up in zoos. Elizabeth also read a book about lions and their cubs. The book's title was A Family of Lions.

To complete her article, Elizabeth watched a television special about lions in the wild. The show was called Living with the Lions. The next day she turned in her article. She titled it Let's Talk about Lions.

1. Which of the following titles should be in italics?

- (A) The Panther's Roar
- (B) City Lions
- (C) Living with the Lions
- (D) Let's Talk about Lions

2. Which of the following titles should be in quotation marks?

- (F) The Panther's Roar
- (G) The Lion King
- (H) City Lions
- (J) Animal Antics

3. A Family of Lions should be italicized because it is the title of _____.

- (A) a short story
- (B) a book
- (C) an article
- (D) a television show

4. The title of Elizabeth's article, Let's Talk about Lions, should look like which of the choices below?

- (F) Let's Talk about Lions
- (G) Let's Talk "about Lions"
- (H) Let's Talk about Lions
- (J) "Let's Talk about Lions"

5. The television show that Elizabeth watched should be written this way.

- (A) "Living with the Lions"
- (B) "Living With The Lions"
- (C) *Living with the Lions*
- (D) *Living With The Lions*

STOP

Language Conventions

1.6

Capitalization

DIRECTIONS: Rewrite the sentences below using the correct capitalization and punctuation.

1. **Tyson began singing the star-spangled banner**

   _____

   _____

   _____

   _____

2. **Joe read an article about canada geese in a magazine called migrating birds**

   _____

   _____

   _____

   _____

3. **We sold school supplies to help raise money for the red cross.**

   _____

   _____

   _____

   _____

4. **Abby said yes, I'm really glad you are here**

   _____

   _____

   _____

   _____

DIRECTIONS: Choose the sentence that shows correct punctuation and capitalization.

5.
   - (A) Tell Mrs Jensen I called.
   - (B) Miss. Richards will be late.
   - (C) Our coach is Mr.Wannamaker
   - (D) Dr. Cullinane was here earlier.

6.
   - (F) Will you please take the garbage out?
   - (G) Dont let Rachel forget her chores.
   - (H) she has been reading *Charlottes Web* all afternoon.
   - (J) This house looks like a pigsty

7.
   - (A) "I suggest you go to the library to do research," Mom said.
   - (B) "The world book encyclopedia is a good place to look."
   - (C) "I will help you look in National Geographic when you get home.
   - (D) Your report will be perfect when your done," Mom insisted.

8.
   - (F) Joel hurt his wrist, yesterday while playing hockey.
   - (G) However, he scored three goals in the process.
   - (H) He will be the champion of patterson Ice Center.
   - (J) Perhaps they will loan him the stanley cup

STOP

Language Conventions

1.7

Spelling

 Clue If you are not sure which answer choice is correct, say each one to yourself. The right answer usually sounds best.

DIRECTIONS: Choose the word or phrase that best completes the sentence.

1. **It is _____ today than yesterday.**
   - Ⓐ cold
   - Ⓑ coldest
   - Ⓒ colder
   - Ⓓ more colder

2. **Nicole _____ the science club soon.**
   - Ⓕ will join
   - Ⓖ joined
   - Ⓗ join
   - Ⓙ joining

3. **Twelve _____ received awards.**
   - Ⓐ woman
   - Ⓑ women
   - Ⓒ woman's
   - Ⓓ women's

DIRECTIONS: Find the word that is spelled correctly and fits best in the blank.

4. **The train _____ arrived.**
   - Ⓕ finaly
   - Ⓖ finnalie
   - Ⓗ finely
   - Ⓙ finally

5. **Please _____ your work.**
   - Ⓐ revew
   - Ⓑ reeview
   - Ⓒ review
   - Ⓓ raview

6. **He is my best _____ .**
   - Ⓕ frind
   - Ⓖ frend
   - Ⓗ friend
   - Ⓙ freind

7. **We can _____ the gymnasium.**
   - Ⓐ decarate
   - Ⓑ decorait
   - Ⓒ decorrate
   - Ⓓ decorate

8. **The store is in a good _____ .**
   - Ⓕ locashun
   - Ⓖ locashin
   - Ⓗ locatin
   - Ⓙ location

9. **Students were _____ for bravery.**
   - Ⓐ honored
   - Ⓑ honord
   - Ⓒ honered
   - Ⓓ honard

STOP

Language Conventions

1.0

For pages 60–66

| Mini-Test 1 |

DIRECTIONS: Combine each group of sentences below into one sentence.

1. **Horses can walk. They can trot. They can gallop.**

_____

_____

2. **The thoroughbred is used for pleasure riding. The standardbred is also used for pleasure riding. The quarter horse is used for pleasure riding, too.**

_____

_____

_____

_____

_____

DIRECTIONS: Choose the answer that is a complete and correctly written sentence.

3. (A) To take good notes.

   (B) Some birds feed early.

   (C) Using a computer.

   (D) Detailed wall chart.

4. (F) Those muffins was delicious!

   (G) Those blueberries is so sweet and juicy.

   (H) We have picked them yesterday afternoon.

   (J) Please have another muffin.

5. (A) Sunday Simon did pitched for the Eagles.

   (B) Simon the Eagles on Sunday.

   (C) On Sunday, Simon pitched for the Eagles.

   (D) Pitched Simon did.

6. (F) Last night at 7 o'clock.

   (G) The third annual school talent show.

   (H) Our class put on the funniest skit.

   (J) Heard my parents laughing,

DIRECTIONS: Choose the punctuation mark that is needed in the sentence. If no punctuation is needed, choose "None."

7. **I ate the whole box**

   (A) ,

   (B) !

   (C) ;

   (D) None

8. **Look out, here comes an avalanche**

   (F) !

   (G) .

   (H) ?

   (J) None

9. **Oranges lemons, and grapefruits are citrus fruits.**

   (A) ?

   (B) ,

   (C) ;

   (D) None

STOP

How Am I Doing?

Mini-Test 1 Page 67 **Number Correct**	**8–9** answers correct	**Great Job!** Move on to the section test on page 69.
	5–7 answers correct	**You're almost there!** But you still need a little practice. Review practice pages 60–66 before moving on to the section test on page 69.
	0–4 answers correct	**Oops!** Time to review what you have learned and try again. Review the practice section on pages 60–66. Then retake the test on page 67. Now move on to the section test on page 69.

Final Language Conventions Test
for pages 60–67

DIRECTIONS: Choose the line that has a punctuation error. If there is no error, choose "No mistakes."

1. (A) The bus will pick us up
    (B) at 830 a.m. sharp for
    (C) the field trip to the zoo.
    (D) No mistakes

2. (F) Sara wanted to adopt
    (G) another greyhound but
    (H) she simply didn't have room.
    (J) No mistakes

3. (A) Clare, Andrea and I
    (B) were next in line
    (C) for the roller coaster.
    (D) No mistakes

DIRECTIONS: Choose the word or words that fit best in the blank and show correct punctuation.

4. _____ we won't be seeing that film.
    (F) No
    (G) No,
    (H) No;
    (J) No:

5. _____ and Russ all went to get their hair cut.
    (A) Max Mikey
    (B) Max, Mikey,
    (C) Max Mikey,
    (D) Max Mikey;

DIRECTIONS: Choose the answer that fits best in the blank and shows correct capitalization and punctuation.

6. **The new mall will open on _____ .**
    (F) may 1 2004
    (G) May 1, 2004
    (H) may 1, 2004
    (J) May, 1, 2004

7. **Do you think we should go swimming,**
    _____
    (A) Sam?
    (B) sam.
    (C) sam!
    (D) Sam.

DIRECTIONS: Choose the answer that shows the best way to write the underlined part.

(1) Can you imagine finding a bottle with a message inside—or perhaps one containing money? (2) bottles may travel thousands of miles in the ocean. (3) Not long ago a child in new york found a bottle that had been washed up on the beach. (4) Inside was 1,700! (5) After waiting a year, the youngster was allowed to keep the money.

8. **In sentence 1, *money?* is best written**
    (F) money!
    (G) money.
    (H) Money?
    (J) As it is

GO

9. In sentence 2, *bottles* is best written

   (A)   Bottles;

   (B)   Bottles,

   (C)   Bottles

   (D)   As it is

10. In sentence 3, *new york* is best written

   (F)   New York

   (G)   New York,

   (H)   New york

   (J)   As it is

11. In sentence 4, *1,700!* is best written

   (A)   1700.

   (B) $1,700!

   (C) $1,700?

   (D)   As it is

DIRECTIONS: Read each sentence. Choose the underlined part that is misspelled. If all words are spelled correctly, choose "No mistake."

12. We <u>should</u> | <u>probly</u> go inside before the
     (F)   (G)

   <u>thunderstorm</u> starts. | <u>No mistake</u>
     (H)   (J)

13. Our dog <u>always</u> | <u>houls</u> at the moon on
       (A)   (B)

   on <u>Thursday</u> nights. | <u>No mistake</u>
       (C)   (D)

14. The <u>weather</u> | <u>forecast</u> for this weekend
      (F)   (G)

   looks <u>postitive</u>. | <u>No mistake</u>
      (H)   (J)

15. Sharon was <u>completing</u> | a <u>puzzle</u> with
        (A)   (B)

   her <u>classmate</u> | Marty. <u>No mistake</u>
      (C)   (D)

DIRECTIONS: Read each answer. Choose the answer that has a spelling error. If there are no errors, choose "No mistakes."

16. (F)   reproduce

    (G)   usualy

    (H)   interest

    (J)   No mistakes

17. (A)   service

    (B)   fountain

    (C)   suceed

    (D)   No mistakes

18. (F)   recieve

    (G)   observe

    (H)   information

    (J)   No mistakes

19. (A)   jury

    (B)   knuckle

    (C)   pollite

    (D)   No mistakes

20. (F)   wildernes

    (G)   structure

    (H)   republic

    (J)   No mistakes

DIRECTIONS: Choose the word that is spelled correctly and fits best in the blank.

21. We need a new _____ .

    (A)   vidio recorder

    (B)   video recorder

    (C)   video recordor

    (D)   vidio ricorder

GO

22. This _____ leads to the gym.

- (F) stareway
- (G) stareweigh
- (H) stairweigh
- (J) stairway

23. Three _____ people lived in the city.

- (A) milion
- (B) millun
- (C) millione
- (D) million

24. Did you finish the _____ yet?

- (F) lesson
- (G) leson
- (H) lessin
- (J) lessan

25. We planted _____ along the fence.

- (A) daisyes
- (B) daisies
- (C) daisys
- (D) daises

DIRECTIONS: Choose the line that has a usage error. If there is no error, choose "No mistakes."

26.
- (F) Me and Paige want to
- (G) go horseback riding this
- (H) Saturday if the weather is good.
- (J) No mistakes

27.
- (A) It wasn't no bother to
- (B) retype that paper since
- (C) I had to do mine too.
- (D) No mistakes

28.
- (F) Please clean up the dinner
- (G) dishes before you start
- (H) watching television.
- (J) No mistakes

DIRECTIONS: Choose the answer that fits best in the blank and shows correct capitalization and punctuation.

29. _____ for the cool camera.

- (A) Thank you,
- (B) thank you
- (C) Thank, you
- (D) Thank you

30. The play will be held on Wednesday, _____ nights.

- (F) Thursday, and Friday,
- (G) Thursday, and, Friday
- (H) Thursday, and Friday
- (J) Thursday and Friday,

31. Our project is due on _____ .

- (A) October 28 2004
- (B) October 28, 2004
- (C) October 28 2004
- (D) October, 28, 2004

32. Please send that to _____ .

- (F) Mankato, Minnesota
- (G) mankato Minnesota
- (H) mankato minnesota
- (J) mankato, Minnesota,

GO

DIRECTIONS: Choose the answer that best combines the underlined sentences.

33. **The driver put the turn signal on.**
    The driver turned right.

    (A) The driver turned right but put the turn signal on.

    (B) The driver put the turn signal on and turned right.

    (C) Turning right, the driver putting the turn signal on.

    (D) The driver, who put the turn signal on, and turned right.

34. **The room was filled with children.**
    The children were happy.

    (F) The room was filled with happy children.

    (G) The room was filled and the children were happy.

    (H) The children were happy who filled the room.

    (J) Filled with happy children was the room.

35. **The mall is new.**
    The mall is near my house.
    The mall is very large.

    (A) Near my house is a mall and it is very large and new.

    (B) Large and new, the mall is near my house.

    (C) The mall near my house is new, and the mall is very large.

    (D) The new mall near my house is very large.

DIRECTIONS: Choose the complete and correctly written sentence.

36. (F) Please help me put out the trash, but before you go to school.

    (G) Please help me before you go to school put out the trash.

    (H) Help me before you go to school the trash to put out.

    (J) Before you go to school, please help me put out the trash.

37. (A) At our school swims my sister on the team.

    (B) The team at our school on which my sister swims.

    (C) My sister swims on the team.

    (D) My sister at our school swims on the team.

38. (F) Will you run for office in the school election next year asked Marion?

    (G) Rowena answered, "I want to, but I am pretty busy."

    (H) "You really should run for president?" suggested Ken.

    (J) Lyle added, I am certain most of the students would vote for you."

39. (A) I read the book *the big brown dog* to my little sister.

    (B) I forgot my *Science Book*.

    (C) Randy ordered *The Joy of Fishing* from the bookstore.

    (D) *Sea dreams* is a book about an adventure in the South Pacific.

72

Final Language Conventions Test
Answer Sheet

1. (A) (B) (C) (D)
2. (F) (G) (H) (J)
3. (A) (B) (C) (D)
4. (F) (G) (H) (J)
5. (A) (B) (C) (D)
6. (F) (G) (H) (J)
7. (A) (B) (C) (D)
8. (F) (G) (H) (J)
9. (A) (B) (C) (D)
10. (F) (G) (H) (J)

11. (A) (B) (C) (D)
12. (F) (G) (H) (J)
13. (A) (B) (C) (D)
14. (F) (G) (H) (J)
15. (A) (B) (C) (D)
16. (F) (G) (H) (J)
17. (A) (B) (C) (D)
18. (F) (G) (H) (J)
19. (A) (B) (C) (D)
20. (F) (G) (H) (J)

21. (A) (B) (C) (D)
22. (F) (G) (H) (J)
23. (A) (B) (C) (D)
24. (F) (G) (H) (J)
25. (A) (B) (C) (D)
26. (F) (G) (H) (J)
27. (A) (B) (C) (D)
28. (F) (G) (H) (J)
29. (A) (B) (C) (D)
30. (F) (G) (H) (J)

31. (A) (B) (C) (D)
32. (F) (G) (H) (J)
33. (A) (B) (C) (D)
34. (F) (G) (H) (J)
35. (A) (B) (C) (D)
36. (F) (G) (H) (J)
37. (A) (B) (C) (D)
38. (F) (G) (H) (J)
39. (A) (B) (C) (D)

California Mathematics Content Standards

The mathematics content standards developed by the California State Board of Education are divided into five major sections. The information within those sections tell specifically what your fourth-grader should know or be able to do.

1) Number Sense

2) Algebra and Functions

3) Measurement and Geometry

4) Statistics, Data Analysis, and Probability

5) Mathematical Reasoning

Mathematics Table of Contents

Number Sense Standards

Grade 4 Mathematics Content Standards

By the end of grade four, students understand large numbers and addition, subtraction, multiplication, and division of whole numbers. They describe and compare simple fractions and decimals. They understand the properties of, and the relationships between, plane geometric figures. They collect, represent, and analyze data to answer questions.

Number Sense

1.0 Students understand the place value of whole numbers and decimals to two decimal places and how whole numbers and decimals relate to simple fractions. Students use the concepts of negative numbers:

1.1 Read and write whole numbers in the millions. *(See page 76.)*

1.2 Order and compare whole numbers and decimals to two decimal places. *(See page 77.)*

1.3 Round whole numbers through the millions to the nearest ten, hundred, thousand, ten thousand, or hundred thousand. *(See page 78.)*

1.4 Decide when a rounded solution is called for and explain why such a solution may be appropriate. *(See page 79.)*

1.5 Explain different interpretations of fractions, for example, parts of a whole, parts of a set, and division of whole numbers by whole numbers; explain equivalents of fractions (see Standard 4.0). *(See page 80.)*

What it means:

- Students should know that fractions are a comparison of two numbers. These numbers can refer to parts of an item and the whole item, such as pieces of pizza compared to a whole pizza. Or the numbers can be items compared to a whole set of items, such as number of oranges compared to the whole crate of fruit. Sometimes the comparison can be simplified, such as $\frac{5}{10}$ is the same as $\frac{1}{2}$. These fractions are equivalent because they are equal.

1.6 Write tenths and hundredths in decimal and fraction notations and know the fraction and decimal equivalents for halves and fourths (e.g., $\frac{1}{2} = 0.5$ or .50; $\frac{7}{4} = 1\frac{3}{4} = 1.75$). *(See page 81.)*

1.7 Write the fraction represented by a drawing of parts of a figure; represent a given fraction by using drawings; and relate a fraction to a simple decimal on a number line. *(See page 82.)*

1.8 Use concepts of negative numbers (e.g., on a number line, in counting, in temperature, in "owing"). *(See page 83.)*

1.9 Identify on a number line the relative position of positive fractions, positive mixed numbers, and positive decimals to two decimal places. *(See page 84.)*

Math   **Number Sense**

1.1

Using Whole Numbers

DIRECTIONS: Choose the best answer.

1. **What is the numeral for twenty five million, three hundred fifty two thousand, twenty one?**
   - (A) 2,535,221
   - (B) 25,352,210
   - (C) 250,352,021
   - (D) 25,352,021

2. **What is the word name for 100,382,004?**
   - (F) one hundred million, three hundred eighty two thousand, four
   - (G) one million, three hundred eighty two thousand, four hundred
   - (H) one hundred million, three hundred eighty two thousand, four hundred
   - (J) one million, three hundred eighty two thousand, four

3. **What is the numeral for three million, twenty eight thousand, fourteen?**
   - (A) 3,028,014
   - (B) 3,280,014
   - (C) 3,028,140
   - (D) 3,208,140

4. **What is the word name for 352,000,001?**
   - (F) three hundred fifty two million, hundred thousand, one
   - (G) three hundred fifty two million, one hundred
   - (H) three hundred fifty two million, hundred thousand
   - (J) three hundred fifty two million, one

5. **What is the word name for 8,437,291?**
   - (A) eight thousand, four hundred thirty seven thousand, two hundred ninety one
   - (B) eight million, four hundred thirty seven thousand, two hundred ninety one
   - (C) eight hundred thousand, four hundred thirty seven thousand, two hundred ninety one
   - (D) eight million, four hundred thirty thousand, two hundred ninety one

6. **What is the word name for 52,052,052?**
   - (F) fifty two million, fifty two hundred thousand, fifty two
   - (G) fifty two million, fifty two thousand, fifty two hundred
   - (H) fifty two million, fifty two thousand, fifty two
   - (J) fifty two million, fifty two hundred, fifty two

7. **What is the numeral for nine hundred ninety eight million, nine hundred eighty nine thousand, eight hundred ninety eight?**
   - (A) 989,899,898
   - (B) 998,899,989
   - (C) 989,989,898
   - (D) 998,989,898

STOP

Name _____ Date _____

DIRECTIONS: Choose the best answer.

1. **Which number is between 456,789 and 562,325?**

   (A) 572,325

   (B) 564,331

   (C) 455,644

   (D) 458,319

2. **Which decimal below names the smallest number?**

   (F) 0.06

   (G) 0.6

   (H) 0.64

   (J) 6.40

3. **If these numbers are put in order from greatest to least, what is the number exactly in the middle?**

   45 55 50 65 30 35 75

   (A) 45

   (B) 50

   (C) 35

   (D) 30

4. **Look at the numbers below. If these numbers are ordered from least to greatest, which answer choice would correctly fit?**

   33,616 255,500 4,580,000 _____

   (F) 887,140,000

   (G) 88,846

   (H) 3,540,939

   (J) 2,193

5. **Which group of numbers is in order from least to greatest?**

   (A) 4, 34, 16, 66, 79

   (B) 13, 24, 35, 44, 65

   (C) 76, 89, 45, 13, 12

   (D) 3, 56, 12, 98, 10

6. **Which of the decimals below names the smallest number?**

   (F) 2.15

   (G) 2.05

   (H) 2.50

   (J) 2.21

7. **What is the correct sign to complete the equation $426.10 ■ $416.19?**

   (A) =

   (B) <

   (C) >

   (D) None of these

8. **Which group of numbers is in order from smallest to largest?**

   (F) 6, 24, 18, 57, 38

   (G) 29, 11, 35, 46, 58

   (H) 14, 21, 34, 53, 82

   (J) 4, 12, 23, 76, 45

9. **Which of the decimals below names the smallest number?**

   (A) 1.90

   (B) 1.21

   (C) 1.09

   (D) 1.18

STOP

Math

1.3

Rounding Numbers

DIRECTIONS: Choose the best answer.

1. What is 458 rounded to the nearest ten?

   (A) 460

   (B) 450

   (C) 410

   (D) 510

2. A number rounded to the nearest ten is 550. When it is rounded to the nearest hundred, the number becomes 600. Which of these could it be?

   (F) 554

   (G) 545

   (H) 559

   (J) 549

3. What is 1,783 rounded to the nearest hundred?

   (A) 1,700

   (B) 1,780

   (C) 1,800

   (D) 1,790

4. What is 788 rounded to the nearest hundred?

   (F) 700

   (G) 780

   (H) 790

   (J) 800

5. A number rounded to the nearest ten is 350. When it is rounded to the nearest hundred, the number becomes 400. What is the number?

   (A) 349

   (B) 359

   (C) 353

   (D) 345

6. What is 365 rounded to the nearest ten?

   (F) 400

   (G) 360

   (H) 370

   (J) 300

7. What is 2,438 rounded to the nearest thousand?

   (A) 2,000

   (B) 3,000

   (C) 1,000

   (D) 2,400

8. What is 4,900,110 rounded to the nearest million?

   (F) 4,900,000

   (G) 4,000,000

   (H) 5,000,000

   (J) 4,900,100

STOP

Math

1.4

Using Rounded Numbers

DIRECTIONS: Decide if the answer should be exact or can be rounded or estimated. Explain your decision.

1. Jose went to the store for bread and milk. His mother wanted to make sure he had enough money, so she added the costs together. How much should she give him?

_____

_____

_____

2. While Jose was at the store, the clerk added the costs of the bread and milk together and included tax. How much was it?

_____

_____

_____

3. Preparing to carpet a floor, Mr. Mason measured the space. How big was the space?

_____

_____

_____

4. The odometer in a car gives a reading of how far the car has gone. How long was the trip?

_____

_____

5. How much shampoo do you use to wash your hair?

_____

_____

_____

6. Tim walked to Amy's house. How long did it take?

_____

_____

_____

7. Lucinda went to the doctor and had her temperature taken. What was her temperature?

_____

_____

_____

8. Robert and his mother need film for their vacation. How much should they buy?

_____

_____

_____

9. Rashawn bought tickets for the movie. How many did he buy?

_____

_____

_____

STOP

1.5

Fractions

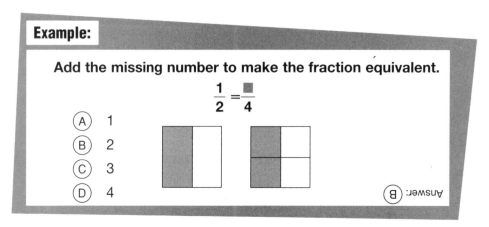
DIRECTIONS: Choose the best answer.

1. Add the missing number to make the fraction equivalent.

$$\frac{3}{4} = \frac{6}{\blacksquare}$$

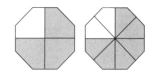

(A) 4
(B) 6
(C) 8
(D) 10

2. Which of these figures shows $\frac{4}{7}$?

(F) 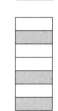   (G)

(H)   (J)

3. Which fraction shows how many of the shapes are shaded?

(A) $\frac{1}{3}$

(B) $\frac{2}{3}$

(C) $\frac{12}{4}$

(D) $\frac{3}{1}$

4. Which fraction represents 4 divided by 5?

(F) $\frac{5}{4}$

(G) $\frac{3}{5}$

(H) $\frac{4}{5}$

(J) $\frac{5}{5}$

STOP

Math
1.6

Fractions and Decimals

DIRECTIONS: Draw a line from the expression on the left to the equal expression on the right.

1. 0.9

2. six tenths

3. 0.4

4. $\frac{32}{100}$

5. 0.7

A. **seven tenths**

B. $\frac{9}{10}$

C. **0.32**

D. **0.6**

E. **four tenths**

6. two tenths equals

   Ⓐ 0.2

   Ⓑ 0.02

   Ⓒ $\frac{2}{100}$

   Ⓓ $\frac{10}{20}$

7. 0.11 equals

   Ⓕ one eleventh

   Ⓖ $\frac{11}{10}$

   Ⓗ eleven hundredths

   Ⓙ eleven tenths

8. five tenths equals

   Ⓐ $\frac{5}{10}$

   Ⓑ 0.05

   Ⓒ $\frac{5}{100}$

   Ⓓ 5.0

9. Which number is not equal to one half?

   Ⓕ $\frac{1}{2}$

   Ⓖ 0.5

   Ⓗ $\frac{1}{3}$

   Ⓙ 0.50

10. Which number is not equal to 1.25?

   Ⓐ one and one fourth

   Ⓑ $1\frac{1}{4}$

   Ⓒ $\frac{5}{4}$

   Ⓓ $\frac{12}{50}$

11. Which number is not equal to one and three quarters?

   Ⓕ $\frac{9}{4}$

   Ⓖ $\frac{7}{4}$

   Ⓗ $1\frac{3}{4}$

   Ⓙ 1.75

12. Which fraction and decimal set below shows equal amounts?

   Ⓐ $\frac{5}{10}$ and 0.5

   Ⓑ $\frac{3}{4}$ and 0.34

   Ⓒ $\frac{1}{2}$ and 0.25

   Ⓓ $\frac{2}{10}$ and 0.02

STOP

Fractions

DIRECTIONS: Choose the best answer.

1. **What picture shows a fraction equivalent to $\frac{3}{10}$?**

   Ⓐ

   Ⓑ

   Ⓒ

   Ⓓ

Use the number line for exercises 2 and 3.

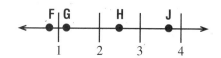

2. **What point represents $\frac{3}{4}$?**

   Ⓕ F

   Ⓖ G

   Ⓗ H

   Ⓙ J

3. **What point represents $2\frac{1}{2}$?**

   Ⓐ F

   Ⓑ G

   Ⓒ H

   Ⓓ J

4. **What fraction of this shape is shaded?**

   Ⓕ $\frac{1}{2}$

   Ⓖ $\frac{3}{11}$

   Ⓗ $\frac{1}{3}$

   Ⓙ $\frac{2}{3}$

5. **Which fraction tells how much of this figure is shaded?**

   Ⓐ $\frac{2}{3}$

   Ⓑ $\frac{3}{4}$

   Ⓒ $\frac{1}{4}$

   Ⓓ $\frac{5}{8}$

6. **Which fraction shows how many of the shapes are shaded?**

   Ⓕ $\frac{1}{6}$

   Ⓖ $\frac{3}{5}$

   Ⓗ $\frac{7}{10}$

   Ⓙ $\frac{1}{2}$

STOP

Math
1.8

Negative Numbers

DIRECTIONS: Use the number line for numbers 1 and 2.

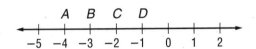

1. **Which letter is at −1 on the number line?**
   - (A) A
   - (B) B
   - (C) C
   - (D) D

2. **Which letter is at −4 on the number line?**
   - (F) A
   - (G) B
   - (H) C
   - (J) D

DIRECTIONS: Choose the best answer.

3. **Which number is not greater than −3?**
   - (A) 4
   - (B) 0
   - (C) −2
   - (D) −4

4. **Which statement represents losing $5?**
   - (F) 5
   - (G) 0
   - (H) −5
   - (J) 10

5. **Which temperature is coldest?**
   - (A) −4
   - (B) 0
   - (C) −2
   - (D) 4

6. **Which statement represents a loss of 3 yards?**
   - (F) −3
   - (G) 0
   - (H) 3
   - (J) +3

DIRECTIONS: Use the thermometer for numbers 7 and 8.

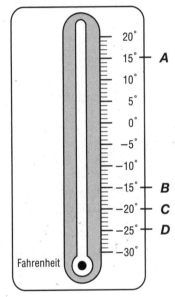

7. **Which letter on the thermometer represents −15°?**
   - (A) A
   - (B) B
   - (C) C
   - (D) D

8. **Which letter on the thermometer represents −25°?**
   - (F) A
   - (G) B
   - (H) C
   - (J) D

STOP

Name _____   Date _____

1.9

Using a Number Line

DIRECTIONS: Use the number line for all the questions.

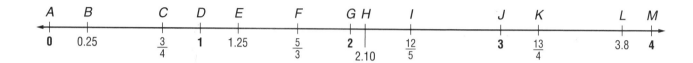

1. **3.5 would fall between which two letters?**

   Ⓐ B and C

   Ⓑ E and F

   Ⓒ H and I

   Ⓓ K and L

2. **How does 1.75 compare to $\frac{17}{5}$?**

   Ⓕ less than

   Ⓖ same as

   Ⓗ greater than

   Ⓙ can't compare because one is a decimal and one is a fraction

3. **Which letter represents 3.25?**

   Ⓐ C

   Ⓑ E

   Ⓒ I

   Ⓓ K

4. **Which letter represents $\frac{21}{10}$?**

   Ⓕ F

   Ⓖ G

   Ⓗ H

   Ⓙ I

5. **1.43 would fall between which two letters?**

   Ⓐ B and C

   Ⓑ E and F

   Ⓒ H and I

   Ⓓ K and L

6. **$\frac{1}{3}$ would fall between which two letters?**

   Ⓕ B and C

   Ⓖ E and F

   Ⓗ H and I

   Ⓙ K and L

7. **$2\frac{7}{8}$ would fall between which two letters?**

   Ⓐ G and H

   Ⓑ H and I

   Ⓒ I and J

   Ⓓ none of these

8. **Which letter represents $1\frac{2}{3}$?**

   Ⓕ D

   Ⓖ E

   Ⓗ F

   Ⓙ G

STOP

Math

1.0

For pages 76–84

Mini-Test 1

1. **Look at the different values. Put the values in order from least (1) to greatest (4).**

_____ Weight of the largest ice cream sundae: 33,616 pounds

_____ Area of the United States: 3,540,939 square miles

_____ Average number of people in the United States watching TV during prime time: 94,900,000 people

_____ Greatest speed of the fastest airplane: 2,193 mph

2. **Round the following values to the place indicated.**

Greatest speed of the fastest animal (the peregrine falcon): 217 mph (tens)

_____

Largest number of pieces in a jigsaw puzzle: 61,752 pieces (thousands)

_____

Amount of food eaten by a wild elephant in one year: 255,500 pounds (hundred thousand)

_____

3. **Write seventy one hundredths as a fraction and as a decimal.**

_____

4. **On a number line, is $\frac{2}{3}$ to the right or left of $\frac{1}{2}$?**

_____

DIRECTIONS: In questions 5–8, the numbers at the left have been rounded. You are given the place to which each number was rounded. Choose the number that could be the original number.

5. **2,000 (nearest 1,000)**

  (A) 1,897

  (B) 1,438

  (C) 1,280

  (D) 2,600

6. **40 (nearest 10)**

  (F) 27

  (G) 32

  (H) 37

  (J) 45

7. **768,200 (nearest 100)**

  (A) 768,290

  (B) 768,220

  (C) 769,199

  (D) 768,000

8. **Joaquim is eating a pizza. The pizza has eight slices and Joaquim eats five. What fraction of the pizza did Joaquim eat?**

  (F) $\frac{1}{8}$

  (G) $\frac{3}{8}$

  (H) $\frac{2}{8}$

  (J) $\frac{5}{8}$

STOP

Number Sense Standards

2.0 Students extend their use and understanding of whole numbers to the addition and subtraction of simple decimals:

2.1 Estimate and compute the sum or difference of whole numbers and positive decimals to two places. *(See page 87.)*

2.2 Round two-place decimals to one decimal or the nearest whole number and judge the reasonableness of the rounded answer. *(See page 88.)*

Math

2.1

Addition and Subtraction

 Clue The answer in an addition problem is always larger than the numbers being added. The answer in a subtraction problem is always smaller than the larger number in the problem.

DIRECTIONS: Choose the best answer.

1. Find 6.89 + 3.00.
   - (A) 3.89
   - (B) 3.98
   - (C) 0.88
   - (D) 9.89

2. Find 925 − 6.
   - (F) 919
   - (G) 931
   - (H) 325
   - (J) 1,225

3. Find 794 − 318.
   - (A) 384
   - (B) 484
   - (C) 476
   - (D) 1,112

4. Last week, the snack bar at the pool sold 1,024 hot dogs. This week, it sold 1,155 hot dogs. What was the total number of hot dogs served for the two weeks?
   - (F) 131
   - (G) 1,179
   - (H) 2,079
   - (J) 2,179

5. Use estimation to find which problem will have the greatest answer.
   - (A) 480 − 73
   - (B) 515 − 325
   - (C) 999 − 777
   - (D) 895 − 555

6. Alessandro's fourth-grade class was having its class party. There are 120 fourth-graders, but 5 were absent that day. How many students attended the class party?
   - (F) 115
   - (G) 125
   - (H) 24
   - (J) 105

7. Seven plus what number equals 71?
   - (A) 10
   - (B) 78
   - (C) 64
   - (D) 1

8. Find 1.5 + 2.9.
   - (F) 1.4
   - (G) 4.4
   - (H) 1.19
   - (J) 3.4

STOP

Math

2.2

Rounding Numbers

DIRECTIONS: Choose the best answer.

1. **What is $73.52 rounded to the nearest dollar?**

   (A) $73.50

   (B) $74.00

   (C) $73.00

   (D) $75.00

2. **Round 0.42 to the nearest tenth.**

   (F) 0.42

   (G) 0.5

   (H) 1.0

   (J) 0.4

3. **Round 0.87 to the nearest tenth.**

   (A) 0.9

   (B) 0.8

   (C) 1.0

   (D) 0.7

4. **Round 1.15 to the nearest whole number.**

   (F) 1.2

   (G) 1.1

   (H) 1.0

   (J) 2.0

5. **Round 6.79 to the nearest whole number.**

   (A) 6.0

   (B) 7.0

   (C) 6.7

   (D) 6.8

6. **Round 5.81 to the nearest tenth.**

   (F) 6.0

   (G) 5.0

   (H) 5.8

   (J) 5.9

7. **Round 1.35 to the nearest tenth.**

   (A) 1.4

   (B) 1.3

   (C) 1.0

   (D) 2.0

8. **Round 6.98 to the nearest tenth.**

   (F) 6.0

   (G) 7.0

   (H) 6.8

   (J) 6.9

9. **Round 1.76 to the nearest whole number.**

   (A) 1.7

   (B) 1.6

   (C) 1.0

   (D) 2.0

10. **Round 3.13 to the nearest tenth.**

   (F) 3.1

   (G) 3.2

   (H) 3.0

   (J) 4.0

STOP

Math

2.0

Mini-Test 2

For pages 87–88

DIRECTIONS: Choose the best answer.

1. Find 31 +25.
   - (A) 32
   - (B) 114
   - (C) 56
   - (D) 124

2. Find 78 +46.
   - (F) 32
   - (G) 114
   - (H) 122
   - (J) 124

3. Find 0.4 −0.4.
   - (A) 0
   - (B) 0.8
   - (C) 0.04
   - (D) 1

4. Find 8.56 −7.59.
   - (F) 9.7
   - (G) 1.07
   - (H) 0.95
   - (J) 0.97

5. To be allowed into the deep end of the neighborhood pool, children must swim 12 laps across the shallow end without stopping. If Jessica has completed 8 laps, how many more laps must she swim to pass the test?
   - (A) 3
   - (B) 4
   - (C) 8
   - (D) 12

6. Use estimation to find which problem will have the greatest answer.
   - (F) 357 − 63
   - (G) 615 − 485
   - (H) 888 − 666
   - (J) 915 − 769

7. Ross and his sister combine their money to buy a new game. Ross has $7.48 and his sister has $8.31. How much money do they have in all?
   - (A) $0.83
   - (B) $15.79
   - (C) $16.89
   - (D) $1.17

8. Round 0.47 to the tenths place.

   _____

9. Round 0.85 to the tenths place.

   _____

10. Round 0.32 to the nearest whole number.

   _____

11. Round 5.55 to the nearest whole number.

   _____

12. Round 19.45 to the nearest whole number.

   _____

STOP

Number Sense Standards

3.0 Students solve problems involving addition, subtraction, multiplication, and division of whole numbers and understand the relationships among the operations:

3.1 Demonstrate an understanding of, and the ability to use, standard algorithms for the addition and subtraction of multidigit numbers. *(See page 91.)*

What it means:

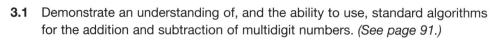

- Students should be able to add and subtract multidigit numbers in a step-by-step manner.

3.2 Demonstrate an understanding of, and the ability to use, standard algorithms for multiplying a multidigit number by a two-digit number and for dividing a multidigit number by a one-digit number; use relationships between them to simplify computations and to check results. *(See page 92.)*

What it means:

- Students should be able to multiply multidigit numbers in a step-by-step manner.
- Students should be able to check an answer by estimating a product by rounding or comparing to known multiplication facts.

3.3 Solve problems involving multiplication of multidigit numbers by two-digit numbers. *(See page 93.)*

3.4 Solve problems involving division of multidigit numbers by one-digit numbers. *(See page 94.)*

Math

3.1

Addition and Subtraction

DIRECTIONS: Choose the best answer.

1. **Find 46 +21.**
   - (A) 4,621
   - (B) 67
   - (C) 76
   - (D) 25

2. **Find 24 +15.**
   - (F) 11
   - (G) 9
   - (H) 39
   - (J) 2415

3. **Find 98 −52.**
   - (A) 46
   - (B) 150
   - (C) 9852
   - (D) 33

4. **Find 33 +26.**
   - (F) 55
   - (G) 59
   - (H) 19
   - (J) 7

5. **Find 846 −123.**
   - (A) 846
   - (B) 736
   - (C) 723
   - (D) 733

6. **Find 388 +639.**
   - (F) 911
   - (G) 1,017
   - (H) 1,111
   - (J) 1,027

7. **Find 736 −595.**
   - (A) 141
   - (B) 131
   - (C) 132
   - (D) 261

8. **Find 987 +223.**
   - (F) 1,020
   - (G) 1,450
   - (H) 1,210
   - (J) 1,200

9. **Find 888 −292.**
   - (A) 586
   - (B) 596
   - (C) 1,180
   - (D) 576

10. **Find 123 +1,054.**
   - (F) 1,731
   - (G) 1,177
   - (H) 697
   - (J) 1,687

STOP

Math

3.2

Multiplication and Division

 Clue You can check your answers in a division problem by multiplying your answer by the divisor.

DIRECTIONS: Choose the best answer.

1. **Which of these is the best estimate of 767 ÷ 7 = _____ ?**
   - (A) 10
   - (B) 11
   - (C) 100
   - (D) 110

2. **Find 185 ÷5.**
   - (F) 37
   - (G) 36
   - (H) 180
   - (J) 190

3. **Find 88 ÷8.**
   - (A) 8
   - (B) 0
   - (C) 1
   - (D) 11

4. **Find 46 ×82.**
   - (F) 3,772
   - (G) 3,672
   - (H) 3,662
   - (J) 128

5. **Find 444 ÷6.**
   - (A) 78
   - (B) 63
   - (C) 74
   - (D) 64

6. **Find 12 ×12.**
   - (F) 240
   - (G) 144
   - (H) 140
   - (J) 24

7. **Find 304 ×57.**
   - (A) 361
   - (B) 247
   - (C) 17,328
   - (D) 19,380

8. **Find 42 ÷7.**
   - (F) 49
   - (G) 294
   - (H) 35
   - (J) 6

9. **Find 145 ×32.**
   - (A) 4,640
   - (B) 725
   - (C) 177
   - (D) 4,760

10. **Find 464 ÷4.**
    - (F) 460
    - (G) 468
    - (H) 116
    - (J) 232

STOP

Math

3.3

Solving Problems

DIRECTIONS: Choose the best answer.

1. Find 178 ×84.
   - (A) 262
   - (B) 94
   - (C) 14,952
   - (D) 1,424

2. The area of a rectangular space is found by multiplying the length times the width. If a room is 12 feet by 15 feet, what is the area of the room?
   - (F) 180 square feet
   - (G) 60 square feet
   - (H) 1,800 square feet
   - (J) 300 square feet

3. A store manager ordered 4 cases of juice boxes. There are 6 boxes in each package and 12 packages in a case. How many juice boxes did he order altogether?
   - (F) 24 boxes
   - (G) 288 boxes
   - (H) 48 boxes
   - (J) 72 boxes

4. A truck driver makes 23 trips each month. Each trip is 576 miles long. How many miles does the truck driver travel in a month?
   - (A) 13,248 miles
   - (B) 12,248 miles
   - (C) 13,589 miles
   - (D) 14,553 miles

5. A gas station sells an average of 847 gallons of gasoline per day. How many gallons will be sold in a typical January?
   - (F) 10,164
   - (G) 23,716
   - (H) 25,410
   - (J) 26,257

6. A sailboat takes 124 passengers on a cruise on a lake. If the sailboat makes 53 tours a month, how many people ride on the boat each month?
   - (A) 5,789 people
   - (B) 5,499 people
   - (C) 6,845 people
   - (D) 6,572 people

7. Lizzie is trying to figure out the area of her desk. The length is 25 inches and the width is 48 inches. What is the area of Lizzie's desk?
   - (F) 1,200 square inches
   - (G) 1,125 square inches
   - (H) 73 square inches
   - (J) 146 square inches

8. What equation would you use to find out the number of minutes in one week?
   - (F) 24×60
   - (G) $(7 \times 24) \times 60$
   - (H) $(7 \times 24) \times 365$
   - (J) 365×60

STOP

Solving Problems

DIRECTIONS: Choose the best answer.

1. Ms. Fava divided her class of 24 students into groups of 2 students so that each student would have a buddy. How many groups of 2 students were there?

   (A) 2

   (B) 48

   (C) 12

   (D) 22

2. Which of the following will have a remainder when divided by 6?

   (F) 12

   (G) 42

   (H) 36

   (J) 46

3. The school basketball team has scored a total of 369 points during 9 games so far this season. What was the average number of points scored per game?

   (A) 47

   (B) 360

   (C) 40

   (D) 41

4. Terrance collected 182 seashells in 7 visits to the beach. How many seashells did he collect during each visit?

   (F) 29

   (G) 26

   (H) 32

   (J) 23

5. A machine can make 1,504 parts in 8 hours. How many parts per hour can the machine make?

   (A) 188

   (B) 1,496

   (C) 1,512

   (D) 24

6. A group of 32 students went to a basketball game. They went in 4 vans that held the same number of students. How many students were in each van?

   (F) 36

   (G) 28

   (H) 16

   (J) 8

7. The computers will be available for the same number of hours each day for five days. If the computers are available for a total of 30 hours, how many hours are they available each day?

   (A) 35

   (B) 25

   (C) 11

   (D) 6

8. When Iris visited the park, she counted 96 birds in a 4-hour period. What was the average number of birds she counted in an hour?

   (F) 24

   (G) 29

   (H) 92

   (J) 100

STOP

Math

Number Sense

Mini-Test 3

DIRECTIONS: Choose the best answer.

1. Find 32 + 45.
   - (A) 77
   - (B) 13
   - (C) 35
   - (D) 72

2. Find 75 − 66.
   - (F) 11
   - (G) 141
   - (H) 9
   - (J) 97

3. Find 32 × 45.
   - (A) 77
   - (B) 13
   - (C) 1,440
   - (D) 128

4. Tyrone and Lawrence have a total of 26 CDs. They each have the same number of CDs. Which equation would you use to determine how many CDs Tyrone has?
   - (F) 26 × 2 =
   - (G) 26 + 2 =
   - (H) 26 − 2 =
   - (J) 26 ÷ 2 =

5. Find 75 ÷ 5.
   - (A) 15
   - (B) 375
   - (C) 80
   - (D) 70

6. Which symbol goes in the box to get the smallest answer for the equation 150 ■ 6 =?
   - (F) +
   - (G) −
   - (H) ×
   - (J) ÷

7. The only charge to use the neighborhood pool is the $3 parking charge. Which of these number sentences should be used to find how much money the parking lot made on a day when 82 cars were parked there?
   - (A) 82 + 3 =
   - (B) 82 − 3 =
   - (C) 82 × 3 =
   - (D) 82 ÷ 3 =

8. Colleen found 16 shells on Saturday and 17 shells on Sunday. Al found 12 shells on Saturday and 22 shells on Sunday. Who found the greater number of shells altogether?
   - (F) Al
   - (G) Colleen
   - (H) They each found the same number of shells.
   - (J) Not enough information is given to determine the answer.

STOP

Number Sense Standards

4.0 Students know how to factor small whole numbers:

4.1 Understand that many whole numbers break down in different ways (e.g., $12 = 4 \times 3 = 2 \times 6 = 2 \times 2 \times 3$). *(See page 97.)*

4.2 Know that numbers such as 2, 3, 5, 7, and 11 do not have any factors except 1 and themselves and that such numbers are called prime numbers. *(See page 98.)*

Factoring Numbers

DIRECTIONS: Choose the best answer.

1. Which of the following expressions does not equal 12?

   (A) 4×3

   (B) 6×6

   (C) 2×6

   (D) $2 \times 2 \times 3$

2. Which of the following expressions does not equal 54?

   (F) 9×6

   (G) 5×4

   (H) 3×18

   (J) 2×27

3. Which of the following expressions does not equal 20?

   (A) 20×1

   (B) 4×5

   (C) 2×10

   (D) $2 \times 2 \times 4$

4. Which of the following expressions does not equal 48?

   (F) 3×18

   (G) 6×8

   (H) 2×24

   (J) 4×12

5. Which of the following expressions does not equal 36?

   (A) 3×11

   (B) 2×18

   (C) 6×6

   (D) $2 \times 2 \times 3 \times 3$

6. Which of the following expressions does not equal 16?

   (F) 1×16

   (G) 3×8

   (H) 4×4

   (J) $2 \times 2 \times 2 \times 2$

7. Which of the following expressions does not equal 32?

   (A) 4×8

   (B) 2×16

   (C) 1×32

   (D) $2 \times 2 \times 2 \times 2$

8. Which of the following expressions does not equal 64?

   (F) 2×32

   (G) 6×16

   (H) 8×8

   (J) $2 \times 2 \times 2 \times 2 \times 2 \times 2$

9. Which of the following expressions does not equal 72?

   (A) $2 \times 2 \times 2 \times 3 \times 3$

   (B) $2 \times 2 \times 3 \times 3$

   (C) $3 \times 3 \times 8$

   (D) 8×9

STOP

Math

4.2

Prime Numbers

 Clue Read each question carefully. Look for key words and numbers that will help you find the answers.

DIRECTIONS: Choose the best answer.

1. **Prime numbers are numbers whose factors _____.**
   - (A) are less than 10.
   - (B) are greater than 10.
   - (C) are the number and 1.
   - (D) are multiples of each other.

2. **Which of the following numbers is not prime?**
   - (F) 13
   - (G) 23
   - (H) 33
   - (J) 43

3. **Which of the following numbers is not prime?**
   - (A) 37
   - (B) 47
   - (C) 57
   - (D) 67

4. **Which of the following numbers is not prime?**
   - (F) 59
   - (G) 69
   - (H) 79
   - (J) 89

5. **Which of the following numbers is not prime?**
   - (A) 21
   - (B) 31
   - (C) 41
   - (D) 61

6. **Which of the following numbers is not prime?**
   - (F) 51
   - (G) 19
   - (H) 11
   - (J) 31

7. **Which of the following numbers is prime?**
   - (A) 56
   - (B) 57
   - (C) 58
   - (D) 59

8. **Which of the following numbers is prime?**
   - (F) 81
   - (G) 83
   - (H) 85
   - (J) 87

STOP

Name _____   Date _____

Math

4.0

For pages 97–98

┌─────────────────────────────┐
│   **Mini-Test 4**   │
└─────────────────────────────┘

DIRECTIONS: Choose the best answer.

1. **Which of the following expressions does not equal 72?**

   Ⓐ 8 × 3

   Ⓑ 9 × 8

   Ⓒ 4 × 18

   Ⓓ 2 × 2 × 2 × 3 × 3

2. **Which of the following expressions does not equal 24?**

   Ⓕ 8 × 3

   Ⓖ 4 × 6

   Ⓗ 2 × 12

   Ⓙ 2 × 2 × 3

3. **Which of the following expressions does not equal 40?**

   Ⓐ 4 × 10

   Ⓑ 2 × 20

   Ⓒ 5 × 7

   Ⓓ 2 × 2 × 2 × 5

4. **The factors of prime numbers are always**

   Ⓕ 0 and 1

   Ⓖ 1 and the number itself

   Ⓗ 0 and the number itself

   Ⓙ 1 and 2

5. **Which of the following expressions does not equal 28?**

   Ⓐ 3 × 9

   Ⓑ 4 × 7

   Ⓒ 2 × 14

   Ⓓ 2 × 2 × 7

6. **Which of the following numbers is not prime?**

   Ⓕ 19

   Ⓖ 29

   Ⓗ 49

   Ⓙ 59

7. **Which of the following numbers is not prime?**

   Ⓐ 7

   Ⓑ 17

   Ⓒ 27

   Ⓓ 37

8. **Which of the following numbers is not prime?**

   Ⓕ 17

   Ⓖ 43

   Ⓗ 49

   Ⓙ 23

9. **Which of the following numbers is prime?**

   Ⓐ 87

   Ⓑ 89

   Ⓒ 91

   Ⓓ 93

10. **What are the factors of 47?**

   Ⓕ 6, 8

   Ⓖ 9, 5

   Ⓗ 1, 47

   Ⓙ 2, 23

STOP

How Am I Doing?

Mini-Test 1	7–8 answers correct	**Great Job!** Move on to the section test on page 102.
Page 85 **Number Correct**	5–6 answers correct	**You're almost there!** But you still need a little practice. Review practice pages 76–84 before moving on to the section test on page 102.
	0–4 answers correct	**Oops!** Time to review what you have learned and try again. Review the practice section on pages 76–84. Then retake the test on page 85. Now move on to the section test on page 102.
Mini-Test 2	11–12 answers correct	**Awesome!** Move on to the section test on page 102.
Page 89 **Number Correct**	6–10 answers correct	**You're almost there!** But you still need a little practice. Review practice pages 87–88 before moving on to the section test on page 102.
	0–5 answers correct	**Oops!** Time to review what you have learned and try again. Review the practice section on pages 87–88. Then retake the test on page 89. Now move on to the section test on page 102.

How Am I Doing?

Mini-Test 3	7–8 answers correct	**Great Job!** Move on to the section test on page 102.
Page 95 **Number Correct**	5–6 answers correct	**You're almost there!** But you still need a little practice. Review practice pages 91–94 before moving on to the section test on page 102.
	0–4 answers correct	**Oops!** Time to review what you have learned and try again. Review the practice section on pages 91–94. Then retake the test on page 95. Now move on to the section test on page 102.
Mini-Test 4	9–10 answers correct	**Awesome!** Move on to the section test on page 102.
Page 99 **Number Correct**	6–8 answers correct	**You're almost there!** But you still need a little practice. Review practice pages 97–98 before moving on to the section test on page 102.
	0–5 answers correct	**Oops!** Time to review what you have learned and try again. Review the practice section on pages 97–98. Then retake the test on page 99. Now move on to the section test on page 102.

Name _____   Date _____

Final Number Sense Test
for pages 76–99

DIRECTIONS: Choose the best answer.

1. **What is the word name for 46,703,405?**

    (A) forty six million, seven zero three thousand, four hundred five

    (B) forty six million, seven hundred three thousand, four hundred fifty

    (C) forty six million, seven hundred three thousand, four hundred five

    (D) forty six million, seven hundred three, four hundred five

2. **What is the numeral for two hundred forty three million, seven hundred ninety four thousand, fifty-eight?**

    (F) 243,794,058

    (G) 243,794,580

    (H) 243,700,940,058

    (J) 2,043,794,580

3. **Which of these is less than 70 and greater than 58?**

    (A) 54

    (B) 69

    (C) 57

    (D) 77

4. **Which group of numbers is ordered from largest to smallest?**

    (F) 472, 381, 205, 367

    (G) 176, 97, 185, 44

    (H) 274, 301, 283, 42

    (J) 173, 120, 85, 42

5. **What is 3,080 rounded to the nearest hundred?**

    (A) 3,100

    (B) 3,000

    (C) 3,070

    (D) 3,090

6. **What is 393 rounded to the nearest ten?**

    (F) 400

    (G) 300

    (H) 390

    (J) 380

7. **Which of the following situations would be a time when the number should be rounded?**

    (A) writing a check to pay a bill

    (B) setting a time for an appointment

    (C) measuring the distance a car traveled in a contest

    (D) telling someone how long a movie lasted

8. **Which of the following situations would not be a time when the number should be rounded?**

    (F) posting the time that a bus leaves a certain spot

    (G) deciding what time to meet at the mall

    (H) buying ingredients for a recipe

    (J) setting a savings goal to buy something

GO

Name _____   Date _____

9. Add the missing number to make the fraction equivalent. $\frac{1}{4} = \frac{\blacksquare}{8}$

- (A) 1
- (B) 2
- (C) 3
- (D) 4

10. What fraction would represent the two figures combined?

- (F) $1\frac{3}{4}$
- (G) $1\frac{1}{2}$
- (H) $2\frac{1}{4}$
- (J) $1\frac{1}{4}$

11. Which of the following is not equal to 0.5?

- (A) 0.50
- (B) five tenths
- (C) $\frac{1}{2}$
- (D) five

12. Which of the following is not equal to one and three fourths?

- (F) 13.4
- (G) $\frac{7}{4}$
- (H) $1\frac{3}{4}$
- (J) 1.75

13. What fraction of the shape is shaded?

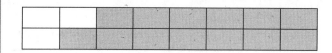

- (A) $\frac{13}{16}$
- (B) $\frac{3}{16}$
- (C) $\frac{3}{8}$
- (D) $\frac{5}{16}$

14. What point represents $\frac{1}{2}$?

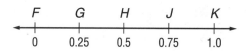

- (F) F
- (G) G
- (H) H
- (J) J

15. How would you represent owing a friend $4?

- (A) 4
- (B) 0
- (C) −4
- (D) +4

16. The temperature was 0° and dropped 10°. What is the new temperature?

- (F) −10°
- (G) 0°
- (H) 10°
- (J) 20°

GO

Name _____   Date _____

DIRECTIONS: Use the number line for numbers 17 and 18.

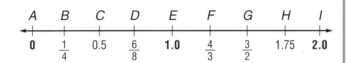

17. Which letter represents 0.75?

(A) A

(B) B

(C) C

(D) D

18. 1.40 would fall between what two letters?

(F) E and F

(G) F and G

(H) G and H

(J) H and I

19. Find 75 +36 +24.

(A) 81

(B) 15

(C) 111

(D) 135

20. Find 7.31 −0.52.

(F) 6.79

(G) 7.83

(H) 7.21

(J) 6.21

21. Round 7.63 to the nearest tenth.

(A) 7.7

(B) 7.6

(C) 7.3

(D) 8.0

22. What is $3.91 to the nearest dollar?

(F) $3.00

(G) $3.50

(H) $4.00

(J) $4.50

23. Find 99 +51.

(A) 48

(B) 141

(C) 150

(D) 151

24. Find 96 −48.

(F) 144

(G) 92

(H) 48

(J) 47

25. Find 354 ×73.

(A) 25,842

(B) 2478

(C) 1062

(D) 427

26. Find 7)7847.

(F) 7840

(G) 1121

(H) 1127

(J) 7854

GO

27. The Bulls played 82 basketball games. The attendance at each game was 6,547. What was the total attendance?

   (A) 536,854

   (B) 80

   (C) 6,629

   (D) 6,465

28. The pet store has 84 birds. It has 14 large cages. There are the same number of birds in each cage. How many birds are in each cage?

   (F) 4

   (G) 5

   (H) 6

   (J) 7

29. Forty-eight cars are parked in a parking lot. The cars are parked in 6 rows with the same number in each row. How many cars are parked in each row?

   (A) 288

   (B) 54

   (C) 8

   (D) 42

30. There are 32 girls in a relay race. Four run on each team. How many teams are there?

   (F) 256

   (G) 40

   (H) 24

   (J) 8

31. Which of the following expressions does not equal 28?

   (A) 2×17

   (B) 4×7

   (C) 1×28

   (D) 2×14

32. Which of the following expressions does not equal 72?

   (F) 2×36

   (G) 3×24

   (H) 4×16

   (J) 6×12

33. Which of the following numbers is prime?

   (A) 33

   (B) 35

   (C) 37

   (D) 39

34. Which of the following numbers is not prime?

   (F) 53

   (G) 57

   (H) 59

   (J) 61

35. What are the factors of the prime number 67?

   (A) 8, 9

   (B) 1, 67

   (C) 3, 19

   (D) 7, 8

STOP

Number Sense Test
Answer Sheet

1 Ⓐ Ⓑ Ⓒ Ⓓ
2 Ⓕ Ⓖ Ⓗ Ⓙ
3 Ⓐ Ⓑ Ⓒ Ⓓ
4 Ⓕ Ⓖ Ⓗ Ⓙ
5 Ⓐ Ⓑ Ⓒ Ⓓ
6 Ⓕ Ⓖ Ⓗ Ⓙ
7 Ⓐ Ⓑ Ⓒ Ⓓ
8 Ⓕ Ⓖ Ⓗ Ⓙ
9 Ⓐ Ⓑ Ⓒ Ⓓ
10 Ⓕ Ⓖ Ⓗ Ⓙ

11 Ⓐ Ⓑ Ⓒ Ⓓ
12 Ⓕ Ⓖ Ⓗ Ⓙ
13 Ⓐ Ⓑ Ⓒ Ⓓ
14 Ⓕ Ⓖ Ⓗ Ⓙ
15 Ⓐ Ⓑ Ⓒ Ⓓ
16 Ⓕ Ⓖ Ⓗ Ⓙ
17 Ⓐ Ⓑ Ⓒ Ⓓ
18 Ⓕ Ⓖ Ⓗ Ⓙ
19 Ⓐ Ⓑ Ⓒ Ⓓ
20 Ⓕ Ⓖ Ⓗ Ⓙ

21 Ⓐ Ⓑ Ⓒ Ⓓ
22 Ⓕ Ⓖ Ⓗ Ⓙ
23 Ⓐ Ⓑ Ⓒ Ⓓ
24 Ⓕ Ⓖ Ⓗ Ⓙ
25 Ⓐ Ⓑ Ⓒ Ⓓ
26 Ⓕ Ⓖ Ⓗ Ⓙ
27 Ⓐ Ⓑ Ⓒ Ⓓ
28 Ⓕ Ⓖ Ⓗ Ⓙ
29 Ⓐ Ⓑ Ⓒ Ⓓ
30 Ⓕ Ⓖ Ⓗ Ⓙ

31 Ⓐ Ⓑ Ⓒ Ⓓ
32 Ⓕ Ⓖ Ⓗ Ⓙ
33 Ⓐ Ⓑ Ⓒ Ⓓ
34 Ⓕ Ⓖ Ⓗ Ⓙ
35 Ⓐ Ⓑ Ⓒ Ⓓ

Algebra and Functions Standards

1.0 Students use and interpret variables, mathematical symbols, and properties to write and simplify expressions and sentences:

1.1 Use letters, boxes, or other symbols to stand for any number in simple expressions or equations (e.g., demonstrate an understanding and the use of the concept of a variable). *(See page 108.)*

1.2 Interpret and evaluate mathematical expressions that now use parentheses. *(See page 109.)*

1.3 Use parentheses to indicate which operation to perform first when writing expressions containing more than two terms and different operations. *(See page 110.)*

What it means:
- Students should know the order of operations (parentheses, exponents, multiplication, division, addition, subtraction) and know that expressions in parentheses are performed first.

1.4 Use and interpret formulas (e.g., area = length $\times$ width or $A = lw$) to answer questions about quantities and their relationships. *(See page 111.)*

1.5 Understand that an equation such as $y = 3x + 5$ is a prescription for determining a second number when a first number is given. *(See page 112.)*

Math

1.1

Variables

DIRECTIONS: Choose the best answer.

1. What number makes this number sentence true? $\blacksquare \times 4 = 8$
   - (A) 1
   - (B) 2
   - (C) 0
   - (D) 4

2. What number makes this number sentence true? $\blacksquare \times \blacksquare = 9$
   - (F) 0
   - (G) 2
   - (H) 3
   - (J) 4

3. What number makes this number sentence true? $\blacksquare \div 2 = 7$
   - (A) 9
   - (B) 5
   - (C) 3
   - (D) 14

4. What number makes this number sentence true? $\blacksquare - 37 = 53$
   - (F) 100
   - (G) 110
   - (H) 90
   - (J) 89

5. What number makes this number sentence true? $\blacksquare \div 4 = 51$
   - (A) 204
   - (B) 240
   - (C) 47
   - (D) 55

6. What number makes this number sentence true? $9 - \blacksquare = 1$
   - (F) 7
   - (G) 8
   - (H) 6
   - (J) 4

7. What number makes this number sentence true? $22.6 - \blacksquare = 8.7$
   - (A) 12.9
   - (B) 13.9
   - (C) 14.1
   - (D) 31.1

8. What number makes this number sentence true? $\blacksquare + 9 = 389$
   - (F) 38
   - (G) 398
   - (H) 12
   - (J) 380

9. The $\blacksquare$ stands for what number? $\blacksquare \times 12 = 36$
   - (A) 6
   - (B) 48
   - (C) 24
   - (D) 3

10. The $\blacksquare$ stands for what number? $3 \times 3 \times \blacksquare = 72$
    - (F) 7
    - (G) 12
    - (H) 8
    - (J) 4

STOP

Math

1.2

Order of Operations

> **Clue**   Remember the order of operations: parentheses, exponents, multiplication, division, addition, and subtraction.

DIRECTIONS: Choose the best answer.

1. Find 3 +(51 ÷3).
  - (A) 17
  - (B) 20
  - (C) 57
  - (D) 54

2. Find (2 ×1,000) +(6 ×100) +(9 ×1).
  - (F) 2,690
  - (G) 2,609
  - (H) 269
  - (J) 2,069

3. Find (8 ×2) +4.
  - (A) 10
  - (B) 14
  - (C) 20
  - (D) 23

4. Find 3 ×(4 +1).
  - (F) 13
  - (G) 15
  - (H) 9
  - (J) 16

5. Find (3 ×4) +1.
  - (A) 13
  - (B) 15
  - (C) 9
  - (D) 16

6. Find 5 +(2 ×3) −2.
  - (F) 19
  - (G) 13
  - (H) 11
  - (J) 9

7. Find (4 ×2) +(3 ×3).
  - (A) 17
  - (B) 12
  - (C) 23
  - (D) 60

8. Find 1 +(5 ×4) +2.
  - (F) 26
  - (G) 23
  - (H) 21
  - (J) 60

9. Find 2 ×(278 +3).
  - (A) 562
  - (B) 281
  - (C) 559
  - (D) 1,668

10. Find (4 ×4) +(7 ×3) +(8 −2).
  - (F) 27
  - (G) 43
  - (H) 39
  - (J) 37

STOP

Math

| 1.3 |

Order of Operations

Example:

Find 24 +[46 −(2 ×11)].

- (A) 92
- (B) 79
- (C) 48
- (D) 748

Answer: (C)

DIRECTIONS: Choose the best answer.

1. Find 9 −(4 ×2).
   - (A) 10
   - (B) 1
   - (C) 7
   - (D) 17

2. Find (9 −4) ×2.
   - (F) 10
   - (G) 1
   - (H) 7
   - (J) 17

3. Find (9 −4) ×(2 ×1).
   - (A) 17
   - (B) 7
   - (C) 10
   - (D) 1

4. Find 48 −[42 −(3 ×9)].
   - (F) 27
   - (G) 9
   - (H) 21
   - (J) 33

5. Find 63 −[(8 ÷2) +(14 −10)].
   - (A) 63
   - (B) 55
   - (C) 59
   - (D) 71

6. Find 800 ÷(200 ×4).
   - (F) 16
   - (G) 150
   - (H) 1,600
   - (J) 1

7. Find 28 +[10 −(4 +2)].
   - (A) 32
   - (B) 36
   - (C) 34
   - (D) 20

8. Find (11 −5) ×(10 +14).
   - (F) 25
   - (G) 74
   - (H) 144
   - (J) 60

STOP

Math

1.4

Using Formulas

DIRECTIONS: Choose the best answer.

Use the shape for numbers 1 and 2.

5 meters

12 meters

1. **What is the area of this shape?**
   (Area =length ✕width)

   (A)   60 square meters

   (B)   34 square meters

   (C)   17 square meters

   (D)   65 square meters

2. **What is the perimeter of this shape?**
   (Perimeter =2 ✕length +2 ✕width)

   (F)   60 meters

   (G)   34 meters

   (H)   17 meters

   (J)   64 meters

3. **What is the area of a square room if each**
   side is 11 feet? (Area =length ✕width)

   (A)   22 square feet

   (B)   110 square feet

   (C)   44 square feet

   (D)   121 square feet

Use this shape for numbers 4 and 5.

4 ft

16 ft

4. **What is the perimeter of the shape?**
   (Perimeter =2 ✕length +2 ✕width)

   (F)   40 feet

   (G)   20 feet

   (H)   64 feet

   (J)   24 feet

5. **What is the area of the shape?**
   (Area =length ✕width)

   (A)   40 square feet

   (B)   20 square feet

   (C)   64 square feet

   (D)   24 square feet

6. **Cara charges 25 cents for a glass of**
   lemonade at her lemonade stand. Which
   of these number sentences should be
   used to find how much money she made
   on a day when she sold 24 glasses?

   (F)   24 + $.25 =

   (G)   24 − $.25 =

   (H)   24 ✕ $.25 =

   (J)   24 ÷ $.25 =

7. **If 1 pound of potatoes costs $2.60, and**
   Miko needs to buy 8 pounds to make
   potato salad, what formula would she use
   to find the total cost?

   (A) $2.60 + 8 =

   (B)   8 − $2.60 =

   (C) $2.60 ✕ 8 =

   (D)   8 ÷ $2.60 =

STOP

Math

1.5 # Understanding Equations

 Clue   To solve two-variable equations, substitute the given value for *x* and evaluate the equation to get *y*.

DIRECTIONS: Choose the best answer.
For numbers 1–4, let $y = 5x + 8$.

1. What is *y* when *x* is 2?
- (A) 15
- (B) 13
- (C) 18
- (D) 21

2. What is *y* when *x* is 3?
- (F) 23
- (G) 7
- (H) 16
- (J) 8

3. What is *y* when *x* is 5?
- (A) 18
- (B) 17
- (C) 2
- (D) 33

4. What is *y* when *x* is 10?
- (F) 23
- (G) 58
- (H) 7
- (J) 18

For numbers 5–8, let $y = 3x - 2$.

5. What is *y* when *x* is 2?
- (A) 8
- (B) 3
- (C) 4
- (D) 2

6. What is *y* when *x* is 4?
- (F) 10
- (G) 12
- (H) 14
- (J) 15

7. What is *y* when *x* is 12?
- (A) 36
- (B) 32
- (C) 40
- (D) 34

8. What is *y* when *x* is 9?
- (F) 27
- (G) 29
- (H) 25
- (J) 23

STOP

Math

1.0

Mini-Test 1

For pages 107–111

DIRECTIONS: Choose the best answer.

1. Find $(14 + 5) + (9 \times 3) - 1$.
   - (A) 30
   - (B) 31
   - (C) 46
   - (D) 45

2. What number makes this number sentence true?

   $$8 - \blacksquare = 6$$

   - (F) 6
   - (G) 4
   - (H) 2
   - (J) 3

3. Find $5 - (2 \times 2)$.
   - (A) 0
   - (B) 1
   - (C) 2
   - (D) 3

4. A rectangular room is 10 feet wide and 14 feet long. What is the perimeter of the room? $(P = 2l + 2w)$
   - (F) 140
   - (G) 48
   - (H) 34
   - (J) 24

5. One pound of hamburger costs $2.50. If Alex needs 4 pounds for a recipe, which formula would he use to find the total cost?
   - (A) $4 - \$2.50 =$
   - (B) $\$2.50 \times 4 =$
   - (C) $4 \div \$2.50 =$
   - (D) $\$2.50 + 4 =$

6. Find $(2 \times 3) + (4 \times 5)$.
   - (F) 14
   - (G) 50
   - (H) 19
   - (J) 26

DIRECTIONS: For numbers 7 and 8, let $y = 19 - 2x$.

7. What is y when x is 3?
   - (A) 25
   - (B) 13
   - (C) 17
   - (D) 10

8. What is y when x is 5?
   - (F) 9
   - (G) 17
   - (H) 24
   - (J) 26

STOP

Algebra and Functions Standards

2.0 Students know how to manipulate equations:

2.1 Know and understand that equals added to equals are equal.
(See page 115.)

What it means:
- Students should understand that an equation consists of two sides that are equal. Just like on a balance, whatever is done to one side must be done to the other side to keep them equal. For example, $a + 5 = 15$. If you add 2 to the left side, you must add 2 to the right side: $a + 5 + 2 = 15 + 2$, $a + 7 = 17$. In all the equations, a still equals 10. Adding the 2 did not change the value of a.

2.2 Know and understand that equals multiplied by equals are equal.
(See page 116.)

What it means:
- Students should understand that an equation consists of two sides that are equal. Just like on a balance, whatever is done to one side must be done to the other side to keep them equal. For example, $5a = 15$. If you multiply the left side by 2, you must multiply by 2 on the right side: $5a \times 2 = 15 \times 2$, $10a = 30$. In all the equations, a still equals 3. Multiplying by 2 did not change the value of a.

Math

Algebra and Functions

2.1

Mathematical Properties

DIRECTIONS: Choose the best answer.

1. **Wallid and Hayden each have $5. Wallid finds $2. How much does Hayden need so they both have the same amount?**
   - (A) $5
   - (B) $4
   - (C) $3
   - (D) $2

2. **If $c = d$, then $c + 7 = \blacksquare$.**
   - (F) $d + 7$
   - (G) $d + c$
   - (H) $d + 5$
   - (J) $d + 9$

3. **If the first frog took 10 hops and then 2 more, how far would the second frog have to hop to get to the same point?**
   - (A) $5 + 4$
   - (B) $6 + 3$
   - (C) $10 + 2$
   - (D) $9 + 5$

4. **John and Keisha each have an apple. If John gets an orange, what does Keisha need in order to have the same thing?**
   - (F) apple
   - (G) banana
   - (H) strawberry
   - (J) orange

5. **If $a = b$, then $a + 10 = b + \blacksquare$.**
   - (A) a
   - (B) b
   - (C) 10
   - (D) 7

6. **If $c = d$, then $c + 4 = \blacksquare$.**
   - (F) $d + 4$
   - (G) $d + c$
   - (H) 4
   - (J) d

7. **If $a = b$, then $a + 12 = b + \blacksquare$.**
   - (A) 10
   - (B) 12
   - (C) a
   - (D) b

8. **If $c = d$, then $c + 15 = \blacksquare + 15$.**
   - (F) 15
   - (G) c
   - (H) d
   - (J) 5

9. **If $a = b$, then $a + 3 = \blacksquare$.**
   - (A) $b + 1$
   - (B) $b + a$
   - (C) $b + 3$
   - (D) $b + 5$

STOP

Math   **Algebra and Functions**

Mathematical Properties

Clue — Remember that to keep an equation equal, whatever is done to one side must be done to the other.

DIRECTIONS: Choose the best answer.

1. If $a = b$, then $a \times 16 = b \times \blacksquare$.
   - (A) 16
   - (B) b
   - (C) 6
   - (D) a

2. If $a = b$, then $a \times 5 = \blacksquare \times 5$.
   - (F) 5
   - (G) b
   - (H) 1
   - (J) a

3. There are 12 cans of fruit per case. If there are three cases of peaches on the shelf, how many cases of pears are needed so there are 36 cans of each type of fruit?
   - (A) 12
   - (B) 36
   - (C) 3
   - (D) 1

4. If $a = b$, then $a \times 9 = b \times \blacksquare$.
   - (F) 9
   - (G) a
   - (H) b
   - (J) 5

5. If $a = b$, then $a \times \blacksquare = b \times 15$.
   - (A) a
   - (B) b
   - (C) 7
   - (D) 15

6. If $a = b$, then $a \times 2 = b \times \blacksquare$.
   - (F) 1
   - (G) 2
   - (H) a
   - (J) b

7. If $a = b$, then $\blacksquare \times 3 = b \times 3$.
   - (A) a
   - (B) b
   - (C) 3
   - (D) 6

8. If $a = b$, then $a \times 18 = b \times \blacksquare$.
   - (F) a
   - (G) b
   - (H) 18
   - (J) 9

STOP

Math

2.0

For pages 115–116

Mini-Test 2

DIRECTIONS: Choose the best answer.

1. Gloria and Eloise are in school seven hours each day. Gloria goes to school every day one week. How many days does Eloise have to go to school to spend the same amount of time there as Gloria?

   (A) 13
   (B) 5
   (C) 6
   (D) 35

2. If $a = b$, then $a + 2 = $ ■.

   (F) a
   (G) b
   (H) 2
   (J) $b + 2$

3. If $c = d$, then $c + 8 = d + $ ■.

   (A) 8
   (B) c
   (C) d
   (D) 6

4. If Frankie and Lin each have $3 and Frankie earns $2, how much does Lin need to earn to have the same amount as Frankie?

   (F) $3
   (G) $2
   (H) $5
   (J) $8

5. If $a = b$, then $a + 6 = b + $ ■.

   (A) 4
   (B) a
   (C) b
   (D) 6

6. If $a = b$, then $a \times 12 = b \times $ ■.

   (F) 2
   (G) a
   (H) 12
   (J) b

7. If $c = d$, then $c \times 13 = $ ■ $\times 13$.

   (A) 3
   (B) b
   (C) d
   (D) 13

8. If $a = b$, then $a \times 24 = b \times $ ■.

   (F) 2
   (G) 4
   (H) 24
   (J) a

9. If $c = d$, then $c \times 7 = d \times $ ■.

   (A) c
   (B) d
   (C) 7
   (D) 17

STOP

How Am I Doing?

Mini-Test 1 Page 113 **Number Correct**	**7–8** answers correct	**Great Job!** Move on to the section test on page 119.
	5–6 answers correct	**You're almost there!** But you still need a little practice. Review practice pages 107–111 before moving on to the section test on page 119.
	0–4 answers correct	**Oops!** Time to review what you have learned and try again. Review the practice section on pages 107–111. Then retake the test on page 113. Now move on to the section test on page 119.
Mini-Test 2 Page 117 **Number Correct**	**8–9** answers correct	**Awesome!** Move on to the section test on page 119.
	5–7 answers correct	**You're almost there!** But you still need a little practice. Review practice pages 115–116 before moving on to the section test on page 119.
	0–4 answers correct	**Oops!** Time to review what you have learned and try again. Review the practice section on pages 115–116. Then retake the test on page 117. Now move on to the section test on page 119.

Final Algebra and Functions Test
for pages 108–117

DIRECTIONS: Choose the best answer.

1. Find [28 −(4 ×5)] −4.
   (A) 8
   (B) 4
   (C) 24
   (D) 116

2. What makes this number sentence true?
   45 +■ =78
   (F) 123
   (G) 45
   (H) 33
   (J) 78

3. What makes this number sentence true?
   67 −■ =26
   (A) 93
   (B) 41
   (C) 67
   (D) 26

4. What makes this number sentence true?
   ■ ×20 =640
   (F) 620
   (G) 660
   (H) 12,800
   (J) 32

5. What makes this number sentence true?
   ■ ÷8 =7
   (A) 56
   (B) 15
   (C) 1
   (D) 16

6. Find 3 +(2 ×5).
   (F) 25
   (G) 17
   (H) 13
   (J) 30

7. Find (6 ×4) −10.
   (A) 24
   (B) 14
   (C) 46
   (D) 0

8. Find 15 ÷(5 −2).
   (F) 5
   (G) 1
   (H) 2.5
   (J) 15

9. Find 8 ×(2 +3).
   (A) 26
   (B) 48
   (C) 19
   (D) 40

10. Find (5 +2) ×(4 +3).
    (F) 31
    (G) 16
    (H) 49
    (J) 120

GO

11. Find (2 ×2) −(3 −1).

- (A) 0
- (B) 1
- (C) 2
- (D) 3

12. The Green family's electric bill in September was $35.74. In October, the bill was $8.19 more. Which number sentence shows how much the electric bill was in October?

- (F) $35.74 + $8.19 = ▧
- (G) $35.74 − $8.19 = ▧
- (H) $35.74 × $8.19 = ▧
- (J) $35.74 ÷ $8.19 = ▧

13. Toby's mother drove her car 193 miles and stopped for gas. Her entire trip was going to be 345 miles. How many more miles does she have to drive?

- (A) ▧ × 193 = 345
- (B) ▧ ÷ 193 = 345
- (C) 345 − ▧ = 193
- (D) 193 − ▧ = 345

14. It takes 5 minutes to clean a car in an automatic car wash. How long will it take to clean 7 cars?

- (F) 7 ÷ 5 = ▧
- (G) 7 − 5 = ▧
- (H) 7 × 5 = ▧
- (J) 7 + 5 = ▧

15. A piece of pipe is 120 centimeters long. If you cut off 49 centimeters, how much pipe will be left?

- (A) ▧ × 49 = 120
- (B) ▧ ÷ 49 = 120
- (C) 49 − ▧ = 120
- (D) 120 − ▧ = 49

DIRECTIONS: For numbers 16–19, let $y = 4x − 5$.

16. If $x = 2$, what is y?

- (F) 8
- (G) 3
- (H) 1
- (J) 22

17. If $x = 4$, what is y?

- (A) 11
- (B) 1
- (C) 16
- (D) 21

18. If $x = 12$, what is y?

- (F) 53
- (G) 7
- (H) 43
- (J) 48

19. If $x = 20$, what is y?

- (A) 24
- (B) 29
- (C) 80
- (D) 75

20. If $a = b$, then $a + 5 = b +$ ▧.

- (F) a
- (G) b
- (H) 5
- (J) 10

21. If $c = d$, then $c + 11 =$ ▧ $+ 11$.

- (A) d
- (B) 11
- (C) 1
- (D) a

GO ⟹

22. If *a* =*b*, then *a* +9 =■.

- (F) *b* + 9
- (G) *b*
- (H) *a*
- (J) 9

23. If *a* =*b*, then *a* +16 =*b* +■.

- (A) *a*
- (B) *b*
- (C) 16
- (D) 6

24. If *a* =*b*, then *a* ×4 =■.

- (F) *b* × 4
- (G) *a*
- (H) *b*
- (J) 4

25. If *c* =*d*, then *c* ×11 =*d* ×■.

- (A) *d* × 11
- (B) *c*
- (C) *d*
- (D) 11

26. If *a* =*b*, then *a* ×6 =■ ×6.

- (F) *a* × 6
- (G) *a*
- (H) *b*
- (J) 6

27. If *c* =*d*, then *c* ×19 =■.

- (A) *d* × 19
- (B) *c*
- (C) *d*
- (D) 19

DIRECTIONS: Use this shape for numbers 28 and 29.

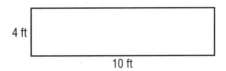

28. What is the perimeter of this shape?

- (F) 80 feet
- (G) 28 feet
- (H) 14 feet
- (J) 24 feet

29. What is the area of this shape?

- (A) 40 square feet
- (B) 28 square feet
- (C) 14 square feet
- (D) 32 square feet

30. The perimeter of a square is 4 times the length of a side. What is the perimeter of a square room if each side is 9 feet?

- (F) 13 feet
- (G) 16 feet
- (H) 81 feet
- (J) 36 feet

31. The ■ stands for what number?

$$■ ×9 =81$$

- (A) 6
- (B) 7
- (C) 8
- (D) 9

GO

32. The ■ stands for what operation sign?

$$63 ■ 9 = 7$$

(F) +

(G) −

(H) ×

(J) ÷

33. The ■ stands for what number?

$$6 × ■ + 8 = 32$$

(A) 4

(B) 7

(C) 3

(D) 5

34. The ■ stands for what operation sign?

$$12 ■ 3 + 7 = 16$$

(F) +

(G) −

(H) ×

(J) ÷

35. Find $13 + [50 − (4 × 10)]$.

(A) 130

(B) 63

(C) 70

(D) 23

36. Find $(18 − 6) × (2 + 2)$.

(F) 48

(G) 36

(H) 24

(J) 22

37. Find $27 − [52 − (9 × 5)]$.

(A) 20

(B) 70

(C) 97

(D) 124

DIRECTIONS: For questions 38–40, let $x = 3y + 6$.

38. What is x when y is 2?

(F) 14

(G) 9

(H) 11

(J) 12

39. What is x when y is 5?

(A) 14

(B) 21

(C) 18

(D) 9

40. What is x when y is 10?

(F) 36

(G) 16

(H) 10

(J) 18

DIRECTIONS: For questions 41–42, let $x = 10y − 2$.

41. What is x when y is 10?

(A) 20

(B) 98

(C) 80

(D) 78

42. What is x when y is 3?

(F) 18

(G) 20

(H) 28

(J) 180

STOP

Algebra and Functions Test
Answer Sheet

1	Ⓐ Ⓑ Ⓒ Ⓓ	31	Ⓐ Ⓑ Ⓒ Ⓓ
2	Ⓕ Ⓖ Ⓗ Ⓙ	32	Ⓕ Ⓖ Ⓗ Ⓙ
3	Ⓐ Ⓑ Ⓒ Ⓓ	33	Ⓐ Ⓑ Ⓒ Ⓓ
4	Ⓕ Ⓖ Ⓗ Ⓙ	34	Ⓕ Ⓖ Ⓗ Ⓙ
5	Ⓐ Ⓑ Ⓒ Ⓓ	35	Ⓐ Ⓑ Ⓒ Ⓓ
6	Ⓕ Ⓖ Ⓗ Ⓙ	36	Ⓕ Ⓖ Ⓗ Ⓙ
7	Ⓐ Ⓑ Ⓒ Ⓓ	37	Ⓐ Ⓑ Ⓒ Ⓓ
8	Ⓕ Ⓖ Ⓗ Ⓙ	38	Ⓕ Ⓖ Ⓗ Ⓙ
9	Ⓐ Ⓑ Ⓒ Ⓓ	39	Ⓐ Ⓑ Ⓒ Ⓓ
10	Ⓕ Ⓖ Ⓗ Ⓙ	40	Ⓕ Ⓖ Ⓗ Ⓙ
11	Ⓐ Ⓑ Ⓒ Ⓓ	41	Ⓐ Ⓑ Ⓒ Ⓓ
12	Ⓕ Ⓖ Ⓗ Ⓙ	42	Ⓕ Ⓖ Ⓗ Ⓙ
13	Ⓐ Ⓑ Ⓒ Ⓓ		
14	Ⓕ Ⓖ Ⓗ Ⓙ		
15	Ⓐ Ⓑ Ⓒ Ⓓ		
16	Ⓕ Ⓖ Ⓗ Ⓙ		
17	Ⓐ Ⓑ Ⓒ Ⓓ		
18	Ⓕ Ⓖ Ⓗ Ⓙ		
19	Ⓐ Ⓑ Ⓒ Ⓓ		
20	Ⓕ Ⓖ Ⓗ Ⓙ		
21	Ⓐ Ⓑ Ⓒ Ⓓ		
22	Ⓕ Ⓖ Ⓗ Ⓙ		
23	Ⓐ Ⓑ Ⓒ Ⓓ		
24	Ⓕ Ⓖ Ⓗ Ⓙ		
25	Ⓐ Ⓑ Ⓒ Ⓓ		
26	Ⓕ Ⓖ Ⓗ Ⓙ		
27	Ⓐ Ⓑ Ⓒ Ⓓ		
28	Ⓕ Ⓖ Ⓗ Ⓙ		
29	Ⓐ Ⓑ Ⓒ Ⓓ		
30	Ⓕ Ⓖ Ⓗ Ⓙ		

Measurement and Geometry Standards

1.0 Students understand perimeter and area:

1.1 Measure the area of rectangular shapes by using appropriate units, such as square centimeter (cm^2), square meter (m^2), square kilometer (km^2), square inch (in^2), square yard (yd^2), or square mile (mi^2). *(See page 125.)*

1.2 Recognize that rectangles that have the same area can have different perimeters. *(See page 126.)*

1.3 Understand that rectangles that have the same perimeter can have different areas. *(See page 127.)*

1.4 Understand and use formulas to solve problems involving perimeters and areas of rectangles and squares. Use those formulas to find the areas of more complex figures by dividing the figures into basic shapes. *(See page 128.)*

Math

1.1

Finding the Area of Rectangles

Example:

What is the area of this shape in square units?

(A) 16
(B) 14
(C) 24
(D) 18

Answer: (A)

DIRECTIONS: Choose the best answer.

1. Which of these shapes has an area of 10 square units?

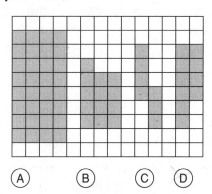

(A)   (B)   (C)   (D)

2. Find the area of the rectangular shape.

(F) 135 ft²
(G) 135 ft
(H) 48 ft²
(J) 48 ft

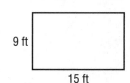
9 ft
15 ft

3. Find the area of the rectangular shape.

(A) 26 in²
(B) 26 in.
(C) 36 in²
(D) 36 in.

4 in.
9 in.

4. Find the area of the rectangular shape.

(F) 25 yd
(G) 25 yd²
(H) 20 yd
(J) 20 yd²

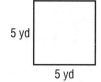
5 yd
5 yd

5. Find the area of the rectangular shape.

(A) 54 cm
(B) 54 cm²
(C) 30 cm
(D) 30 cm²

9 cm
6 cm

6. Find the area of the rectangular shape.

(F) 64 m
(G) 64 m²
(H) 32 m
(J) 32 m²

8 m
8 m

7. Find the area of the rectangular shape.

(A) 234 km²
(B) 234 km
(C) 2,916 km²
(D) 2,916 km

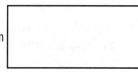
36 km
81 km

STOP

Math

1.2 | Area and Perimeter

Clue Rectangles with the same area can have different perimeters. Remember that area = length × width and perimeter = 2 × length + 2 × width.

DIRECTIONS: Choose the best answer.

1. A rectangle with length of 2 and width of 27 has an area of 54. What is the perimeter?

   (A) 29
   (B) 58
   (C) 25
   (D) 54

2. A rectangle with length of 3 and width of 18 has an area of 54. What is the perimeter?

   (F) 21
   (G) 54
   (H) 42
   (J) 15

3. A rectangle with length of 2 and width of 36 has an area of 72. What is the perimeter?

   (A) 38
   (B) 34
   (C) 74
   (D) 76

4. A rectangle with length of 3 and width of 24 has an area of 72. What is the perimeter?

   (F) 54
   (G) 27
   (H) 21
   (J) 75

5. A rectangle with length of 4 and width of 18 has an area of 72. What is the perimeter?

   (A) 22
   (B) 14
   (C) 44
   (D) 36

6. A rectangle with length of 1 and width of 72 has an area of 72. What is the perimeter?

   (F) 73
   (G) 146
   (H) 71
   (J) 144

7. A rectangle with length of 6 and width of 12 has an area of 72. What is the perimeter?

   (A) 36
   (B) 18
   (C) 6
   (D) 78

8. A rectangle with length of 8 and width of 9 has an area of 72. What is the perimeter?

   (F) 17
   (G) 1
   (H) 80
   (J) 34

STOP

Math

1.3

Area and Perimeter

DIRECTIONS: Choose the best answer.

1. A rectangle has a perimeter of 36, a length of 16, and a width of 2. What is the area?
   - (A) 18
   - (B) 14
   - (C) 32
   - (D) 8

2. A rectangle has a perimeter of 36, a length of 14, and a width of 4. What is the area?
   - (F) 56
   - (G) 18
   - (H) 7
   - (J) 10

3. A rectangle has a perimeter of 36, a length of 12, and a width of 6. What is the area?
   - (A) 18
   - (B) 6
   - (C) 36
   - (D) 72

4. A rectangle has a perimeter of 36, a length of 10, and a width of 8. What is the area?
   - (F) 18
   - (G) 80
   - (H) 2
   - (J) 4

5. A rectangle has a perimeter of 48, a length of 12, and a width of 12. What is the area?
   - (A) 48
   - (B) 144
   - (C) 24
   - (D) 48

6. A rectangle has a perimeter of 48, a length of 10, and a width of 14. What is the area?
   - (F) 24
   - (G) 4
   - (H) 72
   - (J) 140

7. A rectangle has a perimeter of 48, a length of 8, and a width of 16. What is the area?
   - (A) 128
   - (B) 72
   - (C) 8
   - (D) 24

8. A rectangle has a perimeter of 48, a length of 6, and a width of 18. What is the area?
   - (F) 24
   - (G) 72
   - (H) 18
   - (J) 108

STOP

Math

Measurement and

1.4 Using Formulas to Determine Area Geometry

DIRECTIONS: Choose the best answer.

1. A rectangular desktop is 24 inches long and 16 inches wide. What is the area of the desktop?

(A) 16 in²

(B) 80 in²

(C) 384 in²

(D) 40 in²

2. A tabletop is 36 inches long and 24 inches wide. What is the perimeter of the tabletop?

(F) 24 in.

(G) 60 in.

(H) 864 in.

(J) 120 in.

3. A flower garden is shaped like a rectangle. The length of the rectangle is 40 feet and the width is 30 feet. How many feet of edging will be needed to go around the garden?

(A) 140

(B) 70

(C) 1,200

(D) 100

4. A rectangular windowpane is 28 inches long and 24 inches wide. What is the area of the windowpane?

(F) 104 in²

(G) 672 in²

(H) 52 in²

(J) 336 in²

5. Mrs. Sobiech has a rectangular-shaped mirror that is 4 feet long and 3 feet wide. How many feet of ribbon will she need to go around the edges of the mirror?

(A) 14

(B) 28

(C) 12

(D) 16

6. A rectangular picture frame is 32 inches long and 24 inches wide. What is the area of the picture frame?

(F) 384 in²

(G) 768 in²

(H) 112 in²

(J) 56 in²

7. A football field is shaped like a rectangle. The length of the field is 360 feet and the width is 160 feet. What is the perimeter of a football field?

(A) 1,040 ft

(B) 520 ft

(C) 57,600 ft

(D) 28,800 ft

8. To seed the field, the coach needs to know the area of the football field. If the field is 360 feet long and 160 feet wide, what is the area?

(F) 1,040 ft²

(G) 520 ft²

(H) 57,600 ft²

(J) 28,800 ft²

STOP

Math

1.0

For pages 122–128

Mini-Test 1

DIRECTIONS: Choose the best answer.

1. **Find the area of the shape.**
   - (A) 128 yd
   - (B) 64 yd
   - (C) 1,024 yd^2
   - (D) 512 yd^2

   32 yd
   32 yd

2. **Find the area of the shape.**
   - (F) 77 in^2
   - (G) 154 in^2
   - (H) 18 in.
   - (J) 36 in.

   7 in.
   11 in.

3 **Find the area of the shape.**
   - (A) 7,140 cm^2
   - (B) 3,570 cm^2
   - (C) 382 cm
   - (D) 191 cm

   51 cm
   140 cm

4. **A rectangle with length of 3 and width of 4 has an area of 12. What is the perimeter?**
   - (F) 7
   - (G) 14
   - (H) 48
   - (J) 12

5. **A rectangle with length of 2 and width of 6 has an area of 12. What is the perimeter?**
   - (A) 16
   - (B) 8
   - (C) 12
   - (D) 48

6. **A rectangle has a perimeter of 40, a length of 10, and a width of 10. What is the area?**
   - (F) 20
   - (G) 40
   - (H) 50
   - (J) 100

7. **A rectangle has a perimeter of 40, a length of 15, and a width of 5. What is the area?**
   - (A) 20
   - (B) 75
   - (C) 3
   - (D) 40

8. **Sean and Troy are fencing their backyard. It measures 40 feet long by 25 feet wide. How many feet of fencing material do they need?**
   - (F) 130
   - (G) 65
   - (H) 1,000
   - (J) 500

9. **Mr. Owens is buying weed and feed treatment for his lawn that is 65 feet wide by 120 feet long. What is the area of his lawn?**
   - (A) 370 ft^2
   - (B) 3,900 ft^2
   - (C) 7,800 ft^2
   - (D) 185 ft^2

STOP

Measurement and Geometry Standards

2.0 Students use two-dimensional coordinate grids to represent points and graph lines and simple figures:

2.1 Draw the points corresponding to linear relationships on graph paper (e.g., draw 10 points on the graph of the equation $y = 3x$ and connect them by using a straight line). *(See page 131.)*

What it means:
- Students should know that points on a graph can be found by choosing values for x and evaluating the linear relationship to find y. For example, for $y = 3x$, if x is 1, then $y = 3$. So, (1, 3) is a point on the graph for that line. A minimum of two points are needed to draw a line.

2.2 Understand that the length of a horizontal line segment equals the difference of the x-coordinates. *(See page 132.)*

What it means:
- Students should know that a horizontal line segment can be compared to a line segment on a number line. The length is determined by taking the difference of the x-coordinates just like it would be on a number line. The y-coordinate does not change and can be ignored.

2.3 Understand that the length of a vertical line segment equals the difference of the y-coordinates. *(See page 133.)*

What it means:
- Students should know that a vertical line segment can be compared to a line segment on a number line. The length is determined by taking the difference of the y-coordinates just like it would be on a vertical number line. The x-coordinate does not change and can be ignored.

Name _____ Date _____

Math

2.1

Using Graphs

DIRECTIONS: Draw the lines on the graph provided. Label each line clearly.

1. **Draw four points on the graph of the equation $y = 3x + 1$. Connect them using a straight line.**

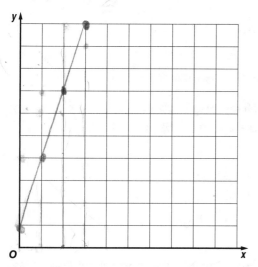

2. **Draw four points on the graph of the equation $y = 2x - 1$. Connect them using a straight line.**

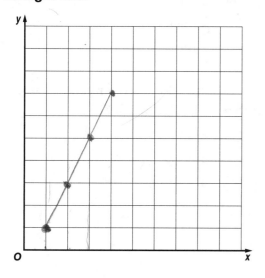

3. **Draw four points on the graph of the equation $y = x + 1$. Connect them using a straight line.**

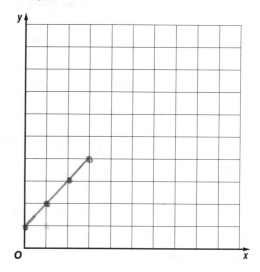

4. **Draw four points on the graph of the equation $y = 2x$. Connect them using a straight line.**

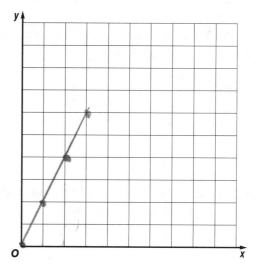

STOP

Math

2.2

Horizontal Line Segments

Example:

How long is the horizontal line segment between (2, 4) and (6, 4)?

(A) 2 units

(B) 8 units

(C) 4 units

(D) 6 units

Answer: (C)

DIRECTIONS: Choose the best answer.

1. **How long is the horizontal line segment between (3, 5) and (7, 5)?**

   (A) 3 units

   (B) 7 units

   (C) 4 units

   (D) 5 units

2. **How long is the horizontal line segment between (1, 1) and (8, 1)?**

   (F) 1 unit

   (G) 8 units

   (H) 2 units

   (J) 7 units

3. **How long is the horizontal line segment between (2, 3) and (6, 3)?**

   (A) 2 units

   (B) 3 units

   (C) 4 units

   (D) 5 units

4. **How long is the horizontal line segment between (7, 6) and (10, 6)?**

   (F) 2 units

   (G) 3 units

   (H) 4 units

   (J) 5 units

5. **How long is the horizontal line segment between (0, 4) and (5, 4)?**

   (A) 2 units

   (B) 3 units

   (C) 4 units

   (D) 5 units

6. **How long is the horizontal line segment between (5, 2) and (8, 2)?**

   (F) 2 units

   (G) 3 units

   (H) 4 units

   (J) 5 units

STOP

Section

Measurement and
Geometry

2.3

Vertical Line Segments

Example:

How long is the vertical line segment between (1, 5) and (1, 8)?

Ⓐ 2 units

Ⓑ 3 units

Ⓒ 4 units

Ⓓ 5 units

Answer: Ⓑ

DIRECTIONS: Choose the best answer.

1. **How long is the vertical line segment between (5, 2) and (5, 3)?**

   Ⓐ 1 unit

   Ⓑ 7 units

   Ⓒ 3 units

   Ⓓ 5 units

2. **How long is the vertical line segment between (7, 4) and (7, 7)?**

   Ⓕ 1 unit

   Ⓖ 3 units

   Ⓗ 2 units

   Ⓙ 7 units

3. **How long is the vertical line segment between (1, 3) and (1, 8)?**

   Ⓐ 2 units

   Ⓑ 3 units

   Ⓒ 4 units

   Ⓓ 5 units

4. **How long is the vertical line segment between (4, 1) and (4, 7)?**

   Ⓕ 2 units

   Ⓖ 6 units

   Ⓗ 4 units

   Ⓙ 7 units

5. **How long is the vertical line segment between (2, 5) and (2, 10)?**

   Ⓐ 2 units

   Ⓑ 3 units

   Ⓒ 4 units

   Ⓓ 5 units

6. **How long is the vertical line segment between (6, 2) and (6, 8)?**

   Ⓕ 2 units

   Ⓖ 6 units

   Ⓗ 4 units

   Ⓙ 8 units

STOP

Math

2.0

For pages 131–133

Mini-Test 2

Measurement and
Geometry

DIRECTIONS: Draw the lines on the graph provided. Label each line clearly.

1. **Draw four points on the graph of the equation** $y = x + 3$. **Connect them using a straight line.**

2. **Draw four points on the graph of the equation** $y = x - 1$. **Connect them using a straight line.**

DIRECTIONS: Choose the best answer.

3. **How long is the horizontal line segment between (5, 1) and (7, 1)?**
   - (A) 2 units
   - (B) 3 units
   - (C) 4 units
   - (D) 5 units

4. **How long is the horizontal line segment between (1, 2) and (4, 2)?**
   - (F) 2 units
   - (G) 3 units
   - (H) 4 units
   - (J) 5 units

5. **How long is the horizontal line segment between (3, 5) and (4, 5)?**
   - (A) 1 unit
   - (B) 3 units
   - (C) 5 units
   - (D) 7 units

6. **How long is the vertical line segment between (4, 1) and (4, 3)?**
   - (F) 2 units
   - (G) 3 units
   - (H) 4 units
   - (J) 5 units

STOP

Measurement and Geometry Standards

3.0 Students demonstrate an understanding of plane and solid geometric objects and use this knowledge to show relationships and solve problems:

3.1 Identify lines that are parallel and perpendicular. *(See page 136.)*
3.2 Identify the radius and diameter of a circle. *(See page 137.)*
3.3 Identify congruent figures. *(See page 138.)*
3.4 Identify figures that have bilateral and rotational symmetry. *(See page 139.)*

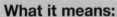

What it means:
- Students should know that
  a. bilateral symmetry means that the object can be divided into two equal halves by only one line through the middle.
  b. rotational symmetry means that any rotation of the object leaves the object looking exactly the same.

3.5 Know the definitions of a right angle, an acute angle, and an obtuse angle. Understand that 90°, 180°, 270°, and 360° are associated, respectively, with $\frac{1}{4}, \frac{1}{2}, \frac{3}{4}$, and full turns. *(See page 140.)*

What it means:
- Students should know that a right angle is a 90 degree angle. This is the angle that is made when two things meet "square," like the floor with the wall, or a table leg with a floor.
- Students should know that
  a. an acute angle is less than 90 degrees.
  b. an obtuse angle is more than 90 degrees.
- Students should know that angle measurements are based on a circle, which has 360 degrees. Therefore, a $\frac{1}{4}$ turn is 90°, a $\frac{1}{2}$ turn would be 180°, and so on.

3.6 Visualize, describe, and make models of geometric solids (e.g., prisms, pyramids) in terms of the number and shape of faces, edges, and vertices; interpret two-dimensional representations of three-dimensional objects; and draw patterns (of faces) for a solid that, when cut and folded, will make a model of the solid. *(See page 141.)*
3.7 Know the definitions of different triangles (e.g., equilateral, isosceles, scalene) and identify their attributes. *(See page 142.)*

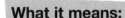

What it means:
- Students should know that
  a. equilateral triangles have 3 equal sides and 3 equal angles
  b. isosceles triangles have 2 equal sides and 2 equal angles
  c. scalene triangles have three sides and three angles of unequal measure

3.8 Know the definition of different quadrilaterals (e.g., rhombus, square, rectangle, parallelogram, trapezoid). *(See page 143.)*

Math

3.1

Parallel and Perpendicular Lines

Measurement and
Geometry

Clue Look at all the answer choices before you mark the one you think is correct.

DIRECTIONS: Choose the best answer.

1. **These lines are _____.**
   - (A) parallel
   - (B) perpendicular
   - (C) right
   - (D) none of the above

2. **These lines are _____.**
   - (F) obtuse
   - (G) perpendicular
   - (H) parallel
   - (J) none of the above

3. **These lines are _____.**
   - (A) parallel
   - (B) perpendicular
   - (C) obtuse
   - (D) none of the above

4. **These lines are _____.**
   - (F) right
   - (G) perpendicular
   - (H) parallel
   - (J) none of the above

5. **These lines are _____.**
   - (A) parallel
   - (B) perpendicular
   - (C) right
   - (D) none of the above

6. **These lines are _____.**
   - (F) obtuse
   - (G) perpendicular
   - (H) parallel
   - (J) none of the above

7. **These lines are _____.**
   - (A) parallel
   - (B) perpendicular
   - (C) obtuse
   - (D) none of the above

8. **These lines are _____.**
   - (F) right
   - (G) perpendicular
   - (H) parallel
   - (J) none of the above

   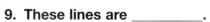

9. **These lines are _____.**
   - (A) parallel
   - (B) perpendicular
   - (C) obtuse
   - (D) none of the above

STOP

Math

3.2

Radius and Diameter

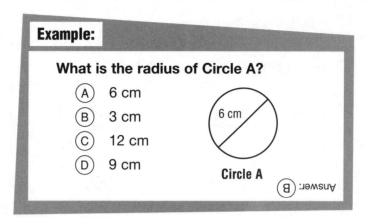

Example:

What is the radius of Circle A?

- (A) 6 cm
- (B) 3 cm
- (C) 12 cm
- (D) 9 cm

Circle A

Answer: (B)

DIRECTIONS: Choose the best answer.

1. What is the radius of Circle B?

- (A) 5 in.
- (B) 10 in.
- (C) 20 in.
- (D) 15 in.

Circle B

2. What is the diameter of Circle B?

- (F) 5 in.
- (G) 10 in.
- (H) 20 in.
- (J) 15 in.

3. What is the radius of Circle C?

- (A) 12 yd
- (B) 16 yd
- (C) 8 yd
- (D) 4 yd

Circle C

4. What is the diameter of Circle C?

- (F) 12 yd
- (G) 16 yd
- (H) 8 yd
- (J) 4 yd

5. What is the radius of Circle D?

- (A) 6 mi
- (B) 12 mi
- (C) 24 mi
- (D) 18 mi

Circle D

6. What is the diameter of Circle D?

- (F) 6 mi
- (G) 12 mi
- (H) 24 mi
- (J) 18 mi

7. What is the radius of Circle E?

- (A) 12 m
- (B) 8 m
- (C) 4 m
- (D) 2 m

Circle E

8. What is the diameter of Circle E?

- (F) 12 m
- (G) 8 m
- (H) 4 m
- (J) 2 m

STOP

Math

3.3

Identifying Congruent Figures

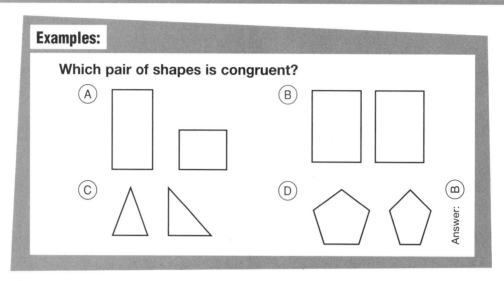

Examples:

Which pair of shapes is congruent?

(A) ▭ ▭   (B) ▭ ▭

(C) △ ◺   (D) ⬠ ⬠

Answer: (B)

DIRECTIONS: Choose the best answer.

1. Which line segment seems to be congruent to $\overline{XY}$?

X ———————— Y

(A) ——
(B) ————————
(C) ———
(D) ———

2. Which pair of shapes is congruent?

(F)

(G)

(H)

(J)

3. Which line segment seems to be congruent to $\overline{AB}$?

A ———————— B

(A) ——
(B) ————————
(C) ——————
(D) ————

4. Which pair of shapes is congruent?

(F) ▭ ▭

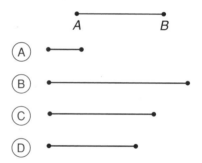

(G)

(H)

(J)

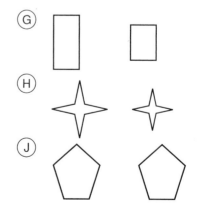

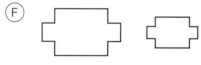

STOP

138

Bilateral and Rotational Symmetry Measurement and Geometry

 Clue Remember that if you fold the paper on the line of symmetry, the two halves match up perfectly.

DIRECTIONS: Choose the best answer.

1. **Which of the figures below does not show a line of symmetry?**

   Ⓐ

   Ⓑ

   Ⓒ

   Ⓓ

2. **Which of these letters has a line of symmetry?**

   Ⓕ **Q**

   Ⓖ **P**

   Ⓗ **N**

   Ⓙ **M**

3. **Look at the letters below. Which one does not have a line of symmetry?**

   Ⓐ **O**

   Ⓑ **T**

   Ⓒ **G**

   Ⓓ **X**

4. **Which of these letters does not have a line of symmetry?**

   Ⓕ **A**

   Ⓖ **G**

   Ⓗ **H**

   Ⓙ **M**

 STOP

Math

3.5

Angles

DIRECTIONS: Choose the best answer.

1. **What type of angle is shown?**

   (A) acute

   (B) right

   (C) obtuse

   (D) none of the above

2. **What type of angle is shown?**

   (F) acute

   (G) right

   (H) obtuse

   (J) none of the above

3. **What type of angle is shown?**

   (A) acute

   (B) right

   (C) obtuse

   (D) none of the above

   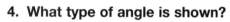

4. **What type of angle is shown?**

   (F) acute

   (G) right

   (H) obtuse

   (J) none of the above

5. **A 180° angle shows how much of a turn?**

   (A) $\frac{1}{4}$ turn

   (B) $\frac{1}{2}$ turn

   (C) $\frac{3}{4}$ turn

   (D) full turn

6. **A 90° angle shows how much of a turn?**

   (F) $\frac{1}{4}$ turn

   (G) $\frac{1}{2}$ turn

   (H) $\frac{3}{4}$ turn

   (J) full turn

7. **A 360° angle shows how much of a turn?**

   (A) $\frac{1}{4}$ turn

   (B) $\frac{1}{2}$ turn

   (C) $\frac{3}{4}$ turn

   (D) full turn

8. **A 270° angle shows how much of a turn?**

   (F) $\frac{1}{4}$ turn

   (G) $\frac{1}{2}$ turn

   (H) $\frac{3}{4}$ turn

   (J) full turn

STOP

Solids

DIRECTIONS: Choose the best answer.

1. Which of the figures below is a sphere?

Ⓐ   Ⓑ

Ⓒ   Ⓓ

2. How many sides does a circle have?

Ⓕ   12

Ⓖ   2

Ⓗ   1

Ⓙ   0

3. Which of the following is not shaped like a sphere?

Ⓐ   basketball

Ⓑ   beach ball

Ⓒ   hockey puck

Ⓓ   golf ball

4. How many sides does a hexagon have?

Ⓕ   5

Ⓖ   6

Ⓗ   7

Ⓙ   8

5. Which of the figures below is a cube?

Ⓐ   Ⓑ

Ⓒ   Ⓓ

6. Which of these shows the top view of the figure below?

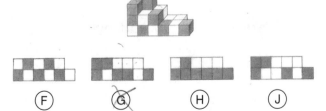

Ⓕ   Ⓖ   Ⓗ   Ⓙ

STOP

Math

3.7

Triangles

Clue Be sure the answer circle you fill in is the same letter as the answer you think is correct.

DIRECTIONS: Choose the best answer.

1. This is a(n) _____ triangle.

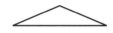

- (A) equilateral
- (B) isosceles
- (C) scalene
- (D) none of the above

2. This is a(n) _____ triangle.

- (F) equilateral
- (G) isosceles
- (H) scalene
- (J) none of the above

3. This is a(n) _____ triangle.

- (A) equilateral
- (B) isosceles
- (C) scalene
- (D) none of the above

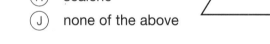

4. This is a(n) _____ triangle.

- (F) equilateral
- (G) isosceles
- (H) scalene
- (J) none of the above

5. This is a(n) _____ triangle.

- (A) equilateral
- (B) isosceles
- (C) scalene
- (D) none of the above

6. An equilateral triangle has _____ sides equal.

- (F) 0
- (G) 1
- (H) 2
- (J) 3

7. An isosceles triangle has _____ sides equal.

- (A) 0
- (B) 1
- (C) 2
- (D) 3

8. A scalene triangle has _____ sides equal.

- (F) 0
- (G) 1
- (H) 2
- (J) 3

STOP

Math

3.8

Measurement and
Geometry

Quadrilaterals

DIRECTIONS: Choose the best answer.

1. **A rhombus with four right angles is a _____.**
   - (A) parallelogram
   - (B) trapezoid
   - (C) square
   - (D) rectangle

2. **A quadrilateral with one pair of parallel sides is a _____.**
   - (F) parallelogram
   - (G) trapezoid
   - (H) square
   - (J) rectangle

3. **A quadrilateral with two pairs of parallel sides is a _____.**
   - (A) parallelogram
   - (B) trapezoid
   - (C) square
   - (D) rectangle

4. **A quadrilateral with two pairs of parallel sides and four right angles is a _____.**
   - (F) parallelogram
   - (G) trapezoid
   - (H) rhombus
   - (J) rectangle

Use the following shapes for exercises 5–7.

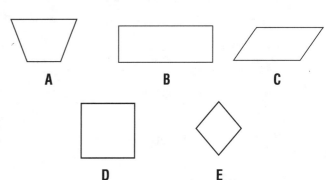

5. **Which shape is a square?**
   - (A) A
   - (B) B
   - (C) C
   - (D) D

6. **Which shape is a parallelogram?**
   - (F) A
   - (G) C
   - (H) D
   - (J) E

7. **Which shape is a trapezoid?**
   - (A) A
   - (B) C
   - (C) D
   - (D) E

STOP

Math

3.0

For pages 136–143

Mini-Test 3

DIRECTIONS: Choose the best answer.

1. These lines are _____.

   (A) parallel

   (B) perpendicular

   (C) obtuse

   (D) none of the above

2. What is the radius of the circle?

   (F) 8 m

   (G) 4 m

   (H) 2 m

   (J) 16 m

3. Which line segment seems to be congruent to $\overline{CD}$?

   (A) •——•

   (B) •————————•

   (C) •———————•

   (D) •—————•

4. Which of these letters has a line of symmetry?

   (F) **C**

   (G) **R**

   (H) **S**

   (J) **F**

5. What type of angle is shown?

   (A) acute

   (B) right

   (C) obtuse

   (D) none of the above

   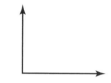

6. How many vertices does a triangular prism have?

   (F) 9

   (G) 3

   (H) 6

   (J) 12

7. This is a(n) _____ triangle.

   (A) equilateral

   (B) isosceles

   (C) scalene

   (D) none of the above

8. This shape is a _____.

   (F) parallelogram

   (G) rhombus

   (H) rectangle

   (J) trapezoid

   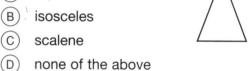

9. A quadrilateral with all sides equal in length is a _____.

   (A) rhombus

   (B) rectangle

   (C) parallelogram

   (D) trapezoid

How Am I Doing?

Mini-Test 1

Page 129

Number Correct

8–9 answers correct	**Great Job!** Move on to the section test on page 146.
5–7 answers correct	**You're almost there!** But you still need a little practice. Review practice pages 125–128 before moving on to the section test on page 146.
0–4 answers correct	**Oops!** Time to review what you have learned and try again. Review the practice section on pages 125–128. Then retake the test on page 129. Now move on to the section test on page 146.

Mini-Test 2

Page 134

Number Correct

6 answers correct	**Awesome!** Move on to the section test on page 146.
4–5 answers correct	**You're almost there!** But you still need a little practice. Review practice pages 131–133 before moving on to the section test on page 146.
0–3 answers correct	**Oops!** Time to review what you have learned and try again. Review the practice section on pages 131–133. Then retake the test on page 134. Now move on to the section test on page 146.

Mini-Test 3

Page 144

Number Correct

8–9 answers correct	**Great Job!** Move on to the section test on page 146.
5–7 answers correct	**You're almost there!** But you still need a little practice. Review practice pages 136–143 before moving on to the section test on page 146.
0–4 answers correct	**Oops!** Time to review what you have learned and try again. Review the practice section on pages 136–143. Then retake the test on page 144. Now move on to the section test on page 146.

Name _____   Date _____

Final Measurement and Geometry Test
for pages 125–144

DIRECTIONS: Choose the best answer.

1. **Find the area of the rectangular shape.**

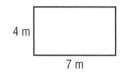

   (A) 28 m

   (B) 28 m²

   (C) 22 m

   (D) 22 m²

2. **Find the area of the rectangular shape.**

   (F) 192 ft

   (G) 192 ft²

   (H) 935 ft

   (J) 935 ft²

3. **A rectangle with length of 4 and width of 9 has an area of 36. What is the perimeter?**

   (A) 40

   (B) 30

   (C) 26

   (D) 24

4. **A rectangle with length of 3 and width of 12 has an area of 36. What is the perimeter?**

   (F) 40

   (G) 30

   (H) 26

   (J) 24

5. **A rectangle with length of 6 and width of 6 has an area of 36. What is the perimeter?**

   (A) 40

   (B) 30

   (C) 26

   (D) 24

6. **A rectangle with length of 15 and width of 5 has a perimeter of 40. What is the area?**

   (F) 75

   (G) 200

   (H) 360

   (J) 99

7. **A rectangle with length of 11 and width of 9 has a perimeter of 40. What is the area?**

   (A) 75

   (B) 200

   (C) 360

   (D) 99

8. **Juan's garden is 6 feet by 8 feet. What is the area of the garden?**

   (F) 28 ft

   (G) 28 ft²

   (H) 48 ft²

   (J) 48 ft

9. **Juan needs to put a rabbit fence around his 6 ft by 8 ft garden. How much fence does he need?**

   (A) 28 ft

   (B) 28 ft²

   (C) 48 ft²

   (D) 48 ft

GO

Name _____ Date _____

Use the graph below for questions 10 and 11.

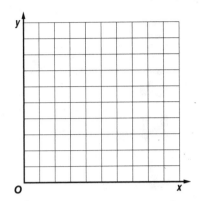

o   x

10. Which part of this graph is labeled incorrectly?

(F) x axis

(G) y axis

(H) the origin

(J) All labels are correct.

11. How long is the horizontal line segment between (3, 5) and (0, 5)?

(A) 4 units

(B) 3 units

(C) 2 units

(D) 1 unit

12. How long is the horizontal line segment between (8, 1) and (7, 1)?

(F) 4 units

(G) 3 units

(H) 2 units

(J) 1 unit

13. How long is the vertical line segment between (3, 15) and (3, 12)?

(A) 4 units

(B) 3 units

(C) 2 units

(D) 1 unit

14. How long is the vertical line segment between (8, 8) and (8, 6)?

(F) 4 units

(G) 3 units

(H) 2 units

(J) 1 unit

15. These lines are _____.

(A) parallel

(B) perpendicular

(C) right

(D) none of the above

16. These lines are _____.

(F) parallel

(G) perpendicular

(H) obtuse

(J) none of the above

17. What is the radius of the circle?

12 in.

(A) 24 in.

(B) 12 in.

(C) 6 in.

(D) none of the above

GO

18. What is the diameter of the circle?

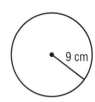

9 cm

- (F) 27 cm
- (G) 18 cm
- (H) 9 cm
- (J) 4.5 cm

19. Which pair of shapes is congruent?

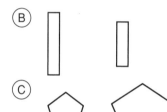

(A)

(B)

(C)

(D)

20. Which line segment seems to be congruent to $\overline{MN}$?

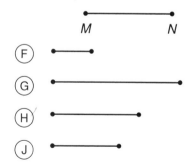

M   N

- (F) •———•
- (G) •—————————•
- (H) •————————•
- (J) •————•

21. Which of these letters has a line of symmetry?

- (A) **F**
- (B) **G**
- (C) **H**
- (D) **J**

22. Which of these letters does <u>not</u> have a line of symmetry?

- (F) **O**
- (G) **T**
- (H) **E**
- (J) **K**

23. What type of angle is shown?

- (A) acute
- (B) right
- (C) obtuse
- (D) none of the above

GO

24. A 90° angle shows how much of a turn?

- (F) $\frac{1}{4}$ turn
- (G) $\frac{1}{2}$ turn
- (H) $\frac{3}{4}$ turn
- (J) full turn

25. How many edges does a trapezoid have?

- (A) 5
- (B) 4
- (C) 3
- (D) 2

26. Which of the following is not shaped like a cylinder?

- (F) can of soup
- (G) tennis ball container
- (H) flag pole
- (J) window frame

27. This is a(n) _____ triangle.

- (A) equilateral
- (B) isosceles
- (C) scalene
- (D) none of the above

28. An isosceles triangle has _____ sides equal in length.

- (F) 0
- (G) 1
- (H) 2
- (J) 3

29. A quadrilateral with four sides equal in length and four right angles is a _____.

- (A) square
- (B) rhombus
- (C) rectangle
- (D) trapezoid

30. This shape is a _____.

- (F) rectangle
- (G) parallelogram
- (H) rhombus
- (J) trapezoid

STOP

Name _____ Date _____

Measurement and Geometry Test
Answer Sheet

1 (A) (B) (C) (D)
2 (F) (G) (H) (J)
3 (A) (B) (C) (D)
4 (F) (G) (H) (J)
5 (A) (B) (C) (D)
6 (F) (G) (H) (J)
7 (A) (B) (C) (D)
8 (F) (G) (H) (J)
9 (A) (B) (C) (D)
10 (F) (G) (H) (J)

11 (A) (B) (C) (D)
12 (F) (G) (H) (J)
13 (A) (B) (C) (D)
14 (F) (G) (H) (J)
15 (A) (B) (C) (D)
16 (F) (G) (H) (J)
17 (A) (B) (C) (D)
18 (F) (G) (H) (J)
19 (A) (B) (C) (D)
20 (F) (G) (H) (J)

21 (A) (B) (C) (D)
22 (F) (G) (H) (J)
23 (A) (B) (C) (D)
24 (F) (G) (H) (J)
25 (A) (B) (C) (D)
26 (F) (G) (H) (J)
27 (A) (B) (C) (D)
28 (F) (G) (H) (J)
29 (A) (B) (C) (D)
30 (F) (G) (H) (J)

Statistics, Data Analysis, and Probability Standards

1.0 Students organize, represent, and interpret numerical and categorical data and clearly communicate their findings:

1.1 Formulate survey questions; systematically collect and represent data on a number line; and coordinate graphs, tables, and charts. *(See page 152.)*

1.2 Identify the mode(s) for sets of categorical data and the mode(s), median, and any apparent outliers for numerical data sets. *(See page 153.)*

What it means:
- Students should know that

   a. the mode of a set of data is the one that occurs most often.

   b. the median of a set of data is the number in the middle when the numbers are put in order.

   c. an outlier for a set of data is any value that is markedly smaller or larger than other values.

1.3 Interpret one- and two-variable data graphs to answer questions about a situation. *(See page 154.)*

Name _____   Date _____

Collecting and Presenting Data

DIRECTIONS: For questions 1–3, use the following information and circle graph.

The fourth grade students at Zinser Elementary were asked to do reports on one of the following five birds: hummingbird, hawk, owl, blue jay, or California condor. Use the graph below to answer the questions that follow.

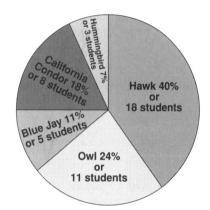

1. **How many fourth graders are at Zinser Elementary?**
   - (A) 100
   - (B) 45
   - (C) 47
   - (D) 50

2. **Which two birds combined get more than 50 percent of the vote?**
   - (F) hawk and owl
   - (G) hummingbird and California condor
   - (H) hummingbird and blue jay
   - (J) hawk and hummingbird

3. **What percent of the vote do the hummingbird, California condor, and blue jay make up together?**
   - (A) 40%
   - (B) 25%
   - (C) 30%
   - (D) 36%

DIRECTIONS: Use the graph below for numbers 4, 5, and 6.

Favorite Vacation Destination

beach	🕶 🕶 🕶 🕶
water park	🕶 🕶 🕶 🕶 🕶
amusement park	🕶 🕶 🕶 🕶 🕶 🕶

Key: 🕶 = 8 votes

4. **For how many votes does one symbol stand?**
   - (F) 2
   - (G) 5
   - (H) 6
   - (J) 8

5. **How many people answered this survey?**
   - (A) $14\frac{1}{2}$
   - (B) 72
   - (C) 148
   - (D) 116

6. **How many more people would rather go to an amusement park than the beach?**
   - (F) 10
   - (G) 12
   - (H) 20
   - (J) 22

STOP

Math
1.2
Modes, Medians, and Outliers

Statistics, Data
Analysis, and
Probability

DIRECTIONS: Choose the best answer.

1. Five students heights are 54 inches, 56 inches, 52 inches, 57 inches, and 53 inches. What is the median height?

  (A) 53 inches

  (B) 54 inches

  (C) 56 inches

  (D) 54.4 inches

2. Bo's turtles weigh 12 ounces, 10 ounces, and 20 ounces. What is their median weight?

  (F) 15 ounces

  (G) 11 ounces

  (H) 12 ounces

  (J) 14 ounces

3. What is the mode of this data: 80, 100, 90, 80, 95, 80?

  (A) 80

  (B) 90

  (C) 95

  (D) 100

4. What number in this set of data would be considered an outlier: 40, 42, 65, 39, 43?

  (F) 40

  (G) 65

  (H) 39

  (J) 43

5. What is the mode of this data: 21, 34, 44, 21, 36?

  (A) 21

  (B) 34

  (C) 36

  (D) 44

6. What number in this set of data would be considered an outlier: 782, 276, 172, 321?

  (F) 172

  (G) 276

  (H) 321

  (J) 782

7. What is the mode of this data: 125, 248, 214, 173?

  (A) 125

  (B) 173

  (C) 214

  (D) There isn't a mode.

8. What number in this set of data would be considered an outlier: 52, 56, 23, 51?

  (F) 52

  (G) 56

  (H) 23

  (J) 51

STOP

Math
1.3

Interpreting Graphs

DIRECTIONS: Use the graph below for numbers 1–3.

Top Countries Generating Hydroelectric Power

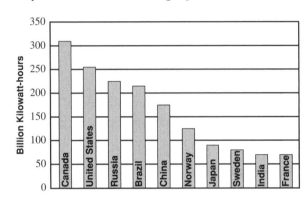

1. **Which country produces the least amount of hydroelectricity?**
   - (A) Brazil
   - (B) China
   - (C) India
   - (D) Canada

2. **Which country produces more hydroelectricity than Brazil and less than the United States?**
   - (F) Russia
   - (G) China
   - (H) Canada
   - (J) Brazil

3. **Which two countries produce about the same amount of hydroelectricity?**
   - (A) India and France
   - (B) Russia and Brazil
   - (C) Japan and Sweden
   - (D) Sweden and India

DIRECTIONS: Use the graph below for numbers 4–6.

Number of Students at Highview School

Grade Level	Number of Students
Kindergarten	♀♀♀♀♀♀♀♀
1st Grade	♀♀♀♀♀♀♀♀♀♀♀♀
2nd Grade	♀♀♀♀♀♀♀
3rd Grade	♀♀♀♀♀♀♀♀
4th Grade	♀♀♀♀♀♀♀♀♀♀♀♀
5th Grade	♀♀♀♀♀♀♀

Key: ♀ = 5 students

4. **How many students attend Highview School?**
   - (F) 275
   - (G) 290
   - (H) 315
   - (J) 192

5. **How many Highview students are fourth graders?**
   - (A) 30
   - (B) 40
   - (C) 50
   - (D) 60

6. **What is the mean or average number of students in each grade at Highview? (round to the nearest one)**
   - (F) 41
   - (G) 46
   - (H) 38
   - (J) 52

STOP

Name _____   Date _____

Math
1.0
For pages 152–154

Statistics, Data
Analysis, and
Probability

Mini-Test 1

DIRECTIONS: Choose the best answer.

1. **What is the least favorite pet in Ms. Paice's class?**

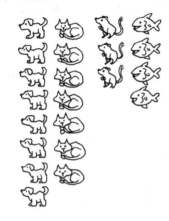

   (A) dog

   (B) cat

   (C) gerbil

   (D) fish

2. **What is the mode of this data: 40, 60, 50, 60, 30?**

   (F) 30

   (G) 40

   (H) 50

   (J) 60

3. **What number in this set of data would be considered an outlier: 437, 509, 864, 474?**

   (A) 437

   (B) 509

   (C) 864

   (D) 474

DIRECTIONS: The graph below shows the cost of a ticket to the movies in five different cities. Use the graph for numbers 4–6.

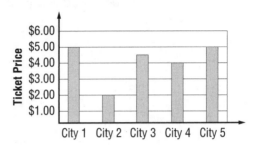

4. **Which city has the cheapest movie tickets?**

   (F) City 5

   (G) City 4

   (H) City 2

   (J) City 1

5. **Which ticket price is found in more than one city?**

   (A) $4.00

   (B) $10.00

   (C) $2.00

   (D) $5.00

6. **How much more does it cost to buy a movie ticket in City 1 than in City 2?**

   (F) $5.00

   (G) $3.00

   (H) $2.00

   (J) $4.00

STOP

Statistics, Data Analysis, and Probability Standards

2.0 Students make predictions for simple probability situations:

2.1 Represent all possible outcomes for a simple probability situation in an organized way (e.g., tables, grids, tree diagrams). *(See page 157.)*

2.2 Express outcomes of experimental probability situations verbally and numerically (e.g., 3 out of 4; $\frac{3}{4}$). *(See page 158.)*

Name _____   Date _____

Math
2.1

Probability

Statistics, Data
Analysis, and
Probability

Venita is making a sandwich. She has white, wheat, and Italian bread. She can choose from ham, roast beef, and turkey for the meat. Use the following tree diagram to answer questions 1–3.

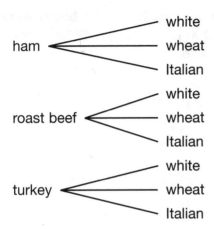

1. How many choices does Venita have?

(A) 12

(B) 9

(C) 3

(D) 6

2. If Venita decides she doesn't want wheat bread, how many choices does she have?

(F) 12

(G) 9

(H) 3

(J) 6

3. Which of the following is not an option Venita can choose?

(A) roast beef on rye

(B) turkey on Italian

(C) ham on wheat

(D) turkey on white

DIRECTIONS: Choose the best answer.

Scott was choosing what to wear one morning. He has jeans or khakis for pants and red, blue, and green shirts. Use the following tree diagram to answer questions 4–6.

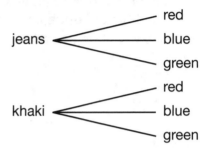

4. How many options does Scott have for outfits?

(F) 6

(G) 3

(H) 8

(J) 2

5. Which of the following is not an option?

(A) jeans with red shirt

(B) khakis with blue shirt

(C) jeans with yellow shirt

(D) khakis with green shirt

6. If Scott decides he wants to wear his blue shirt, how many options does he have?

(F) 6

(G) 3

(H) 8

(J) 2

STOP

Name _____ Date _____

Math

2.2

Statistics, Data
Analysis, and
Probability

Probability

DIRECTIONS: Use the following information for numbers 1–3. In a grocery bag there are 6 cans of tomato sauce, 4 cans of beans, and 9 cans of olives. All the cans are the same size.

1. If you reached into the bag without looking and picked out a can, what is the probability of picking a can of olives?

   (A) $\frac{1}{2}$

   (B) $\frac{1}{9}$

   (C) $\frac{9}{1}$

   (D) $\frac{9}{19}$

2. If you reached into the bag without looking and picked out a can, what is the probability of picking a can of beans?

   (F) $\frac{4}{19}$

   (G) $\frac{1}{4}$

   (H) $\frac{4}{9}$

   (J) $\frac{4}{6}$

3. If you reached into the bag without looking and picked out a can, what is the probability of picking a can of tomato sauce?

   (A) $\frac{1}{2}$

   (B) $\frac{6}{9}$

   (C) $\frac{6}{19}$

   (D) $\frac{4}{6}$

DIRECTIONS: Use the following information for numbers 4–6. A box contains 5 red crayons, 3 green crayons, and 2 blue crayons.

4. If you reach into the box without looking, what is the probability of picking a blue crayon?

   (F) $\frac{5}{10}$

   (G) $\frac{1}{5}$

   (H) $\frac{2}{5}$

   (J) $\frac{2}{3}$

5. If you reach into the box without looking, what is the probability of picking a red crayon?

   (A) $\frac{1}{2}$

   (B) $\frac{1}{5}$

   (C) $\frac{2}{5}$

   (D) $\frac{2}{3}$

6. If you reach into the box without looking, what is the probability of picking a green crayon?

   (F) $\frac{3}{10}$

   (G) $\frac{3}{5}$

   (H) $\frac{3}{7}$

   (J) $\frac{5}{3}$

STOP

Math
2.0

For pages 157–158

Mini-Test 2

Statistics, Data
Analysis, and
Probability

DIRECTIONS: Choose the best answer.

Edison was wrapping a present. He had blue, silver, and gold ribbon and white, red, and black wrapping paper. Use the following tree diagram to answer questions 1–3.

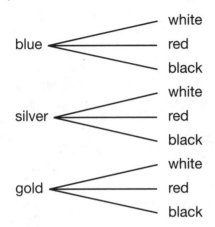

blue — white
blue — red
blue — black
silver — white
silver — red
silver — black
gold — white
gold — red
gold — black

1. **How many wrapping options did Edison have?**
   - (A) 12
   - (B) 3
   - (C) 9
   - (D) 6

2. **Which of the following is not an option?**
   - (F) silver ribbon on white paper
   - (G) blue ribbon on yellow paper
   - (H) blue ribbon on red paper
   - (J) gold ribbon on black paper

3. **If Edison decides not to use the black paper, how many options does he have?**
   - (A) 12
   - (B) 3
   - (C) 9
   - (D) 6

DIRECTIONS: Use the following information for questions 4–6. A bag contains 7 red marbles, 5 green marbles, 3 white marbles, and 2 gold marbles.

4. **If you reach into the bag without looking, what is the probability of picking a red marble?**
   - (F) $\frac{7}{10}$
   - (G) $\frac{7}{17}$
   - (H) $\frac{7}{8}$
   - (J) $\frac{7}{9}$

5. **What is the probability of picking a gold marble?**
   - (A) $\frac{2}{17}$
   - (B) $\frac{2}{7}$
   - (C) $\frac{2}{5}$
   - (D) $\frac{2}{3}$

6. **What is the probability of picking a green marble?**
   - (F) $\frac{5}{7}$
   - (G) $\frac{5}{5}$
   - (H) $\frac{5}{15}$
   - (J) $\frac{5}{17}$

STOP

How Am I Doing?

Mini-Test 1	6 answers correct	**Great Job!** Move on to the section test on page 161.
Page 155 **Number Correct**	4–5 answers correct	**You're almost there!** But you still need a little practice. Review practice pages 152–154 before moving on to the section test on page 161.
	0–3 answers correct	**Oops!** Time to review what you have learned and try again. Review the practice section on pages 152–154. Then retake the test on page 155. Now move on to the section test on page 161.
Mini-Test 2	6 answers correct	**Awesome!** Move on to the section test on page 161.
Page 159 **Number Correct**	4–5 answers correct	**You're almost there!** But you still need a little practice. Review practice pages 157–158 before moving on to the section test on page 161.
	0–3 answers correct	**Oops!** Time to review what you have learned and try again. Review the practice section on pages 157–158. Then retake the test on page 159. Now move on to the section test on page 161.

Name _____   Date _____

Final Statistics, Data Analysis, and Probability Test
for pages 152–159

DIRECTIONS: The graph below shows how many buttons were on the clothing of five students in a class. Use the graph for numbers 1–3.

Number of Buttons

Jason	⦿ ⦿ ⦿ ⦿ ⦿ ⦿
Pat	⦿ ⦿
Nancy	⦿ ⦿ ⦿ ⦿
Paul	⦿ ⦿ ⦿ ⦿ ⦿
Shirley	⦿ ⦿ ⦿

1. Which student had the fewest buttons?

- (A) Pat
- (B) Paul
- (C) Shirley
- (D) Jason

2. How many buttons did the student with the most buttons have?

- (F) 6
- (G) 24
- (H) 10
- (J) 46

3. How many buttons did the student with the fewest buttons have?

- (A) 2
- (B) 6
- (C) 8
- (D) 12

DIRECTIONS: The graph below shows the number of new houses built in a town over a 6-year period. Use the graph for numbers 4–6.

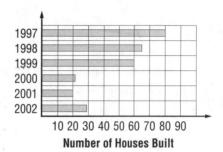

Number of Houses Built

4. In which year were 20 houses built?

- (F) 1999
- (G) 2001
- (H) 2002
- (J) 1997

5. How many more houses were built in 1997 than in 1999?

- (A) 60
- (B) 10
- (C) 80
- (D) 20

6. Between which two years was the change in the number of houses built the greatest?

- (F) 2001 and 2002
- (G) 2000 and 2001
- (H) 1999 and 2000
- (J) 1997 and 1998

GO

Name _____ Date _____

DIRECTIONS: Choose the best answer.

7. **What is the mode of this data: 31, 54, 34, 31, 56?**

   (A) 31

   (B) 54

   (C) 56

   (D) 34

8. **What number in this set of data would be considered an outlier: 882, 376, 272, 294?**

   (F) 376

   (G) 272

   (H) 294

   (J) 882

9. **What is the mode of this data: 521, 482, 146, 371?**

   (A) 521

   (B) 146

   (C) 482

   (D) There is no mode.

DIRECTIONS: Use the following tree diagram for numbers 10–12. Adam was dressing to go out and play in the snow. He had a blue coat and a green coat and red, blue, and gray mittens.

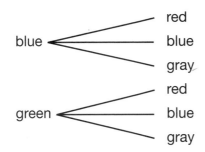

10. **How many options does Adam have for outfits?**

    (F) 6

    (G) 3

    (H) 8

    (J) 2

11. **Which of the following is not an option?**

    (A) blue coat and gray mittens

    (B) green coat and gray mittens

    (C) blue coat and yellow mittens

    (D) green coat and blue mittens

12. **If Adam decides he doesn't want to wear the green coat, how many options does he have?**

    (F) 6

    (G) 3

    (H) 8

    (J) 2

DIRECTIONS: Use the following information for numbers 13 and 14. Amanda had 6 green socks, 8 brown socks, and 12 black socks in a basket.

13. **If she reaches into the basket without looking and picks out a sock, what is the probability of picking a brown sock?**

    (A) $\frac{8}{13}$

    (B) $\frac{4}{13}$

    (C) $\frac{2}{3}$

    (D) $\frac{1}{2}$

14. **If she reaches into the basket without looking and picks out a sock, what is the probability of picking a green sock?**

    (F) $\frac{1}{2}$

    (G) $\frac{3}{4}$

    (H) $\frac{3}{13}$

    (J) $\frac{1}{3}$

STOP

Statistics, Data Analysis, and Probability Test
Answer Sheet

1 Ⓐ Ⓑ Ⓒ Ⓓ
2 Ⓕ Ⓖ Ⓗ Ⓙ
3 Ⓐ Ⓑ Ⓒ Ⓓ
4 Ⓕ Ⓖ Ⓗ Ⓙ
5 Ⓐ Ⓑ Ⓒ Ⓓ
6 Ⓕ Ⓖ Ⓗ Ⓙ
7 Ⓐ Ⓑ Ⓒ Ⓓ
8 Ⓕ Ⓖ Ⓗ Ⓙ
9 Ⓐ Ⓑ Ⓒ Ⓓ
10 Ⓕ Ⓖ Ⓗ Ⓙ

11 Ⓐ Ⓑ Ⓒ Ⓓ
12 Ⓕ Ⓖ Ⓗ Ⓙ
13 Ⓐ Ⓑ Ⓒ Ⓓ
14 Ⓕ Ⓖ Ⓗ Ⓙ

Mathematical Reasoning Standards

1.0 Students make decisions about how to approach problems:

1.1 Analyze problems by identifying relationships, distinguishing relevant from irrelevant information, sequencing and prioritizing information, and observing patterns. *(See page 165.)*

What it means:

- When presented with a math problem, students should be able to gather the correct information, in the correct order, and apply relevant mathematical concepts. For example, given the problem: *Six cases of pears and five cases of peaches are delivered to the school cafeteria. Each case contains 12 cans. The peaches are in 32-ounce cans and the pears are in 64-ounce cans. How many cans of pears are there?* Students should determine that they will need to use multiplication to determine the answer. Irrelevant information includes the number of cases of peaches and the size of the cans.

1.2 Determine when and how to break a problem into simpler parts. *(See page 166.)*

What it means:

- Given the problem: *A room is 8 feet wide and 10 feet long. The piece of carpet I have is 5 feet wide by 7 feet long. What area of the floor will be left bare?* Students should be able to break the problem into parts to solve it. First, they need to find the area of the room and the area of the rug. Second, they then need to find the difference between the two.

1.1

Solving Problems

Sketching pictures may help you answer the questions.

DIRECTIONS: Choose the best answer.

1. Which shape is missing from this pattern?

   ?

(A)

(B)

(C)

(D)

2. If this number pattern continues, what number will come next?

10, 20, 12, 18, 14, 16, _____

(F) 18

(G) 16

(H) 14

(J) 12

3. What number is missing from the sequence shown below?

50, 43, 36, _____, 22, 15

(A) 28

(B) 30

(C) 29

(D) 33

DIRECTIONS: Use the graph for numbers 4–5.

Cheese Production
Percent by Type, 1 Year's Production

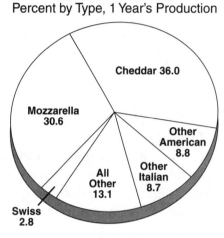

4. Which cheese is made the least?

(F) Other Italian

(G) Mozzarella

(H) Cheddar

(J) Swiss

5. Which two cheeses together make up 66.6% of the year's production?

(A) Other American and Other Italian

(B) Cheddar and Mozzarella

(C) Mozzarella and Swiss

(D) Cheddar and Swiss

STOP

Solving Problems

DIRECTIONS: Choose the best answer.

1. Michelle had $10\frac{2}{3}$ feet of wood. She used 9 feet to build shelves. Which of these shows how much wood she had left?

   (A) $10\frac{2}{3} + 9 = \blacksquare$

   (B) $10\frac{2}{3} \times 9 = \blacksquare$

   (C) $10\frac{2}{3} - 9 = \blacksquare$

   (D) $10\frac{2}{3} \div 9 = \blacksquare$

2. Suppose you had 15 objects and you wanted to put them into 5 boxes. How would you find out the number of objects that would fit into each box?

   (F) divide 15 by 5

   (G) multiply 15 by 5

   (H) add 15 and 5

   (J) subtract 5 from 15

3. What would be a fast way to add the same number 10 times?

   (A) subtract 10 from the number

   (B) divide the number by 10

   (C) multiply the number by 10

   (D) add 10 to the number

4. Rayna wants to buy a toy that costs $1.39. She has the coins below. How much more does she need?

   (F) $1.04

   (G) 69¢

   (H) 70¢

   (J) $1.05

5. There are 12 eggs in a dozen. Which number sentence shows how many eggs are in 3 dozen?

   (A) $12 \div 3 = \blacksquare$

   (B) $12 - 3 = \blacksquare$

   (C) $12 + 3 = \blacksquare$

   (D) $12 \times 3 = \blacksquare$

6. Thomas began a small business selling bags of dried fruit. In the first week he sold 11 bags, in the second week 14 bags, and in the third week 17 bags. If this pattern continues, how many bags of fruit will he sell in the sixth week?

   (F) 29

   (G) 23

   (H) 20

   (J) 26

7. Suppose you knew the weight of a package of meat and the price per pound of the meat. Which of these questions could you not answer?

   (A) What is the price of the meat when it is on sale for 10¢ a pound a less?

   (B) What is the price of 5 pounds of meat?

   (C) What is the price of the package of meat?

   (D) What is the price of the same meat at another store?

STOP

Math

1.0

For pages 165–166

Mini-Test 1

Mathematical Reasoning

DIRECTIONS: Use the graph for numbers 1–3.

Glasses of Water

Monday	⊔⊔⊔⊔
Tuesday	⊔⊔⊔⊔⊔⊔⊔⊔
Wednesday	⊔⊔⊔⊔⊔⊔
Thursday	⊔⊔⊔⊔⊔⊔⊔⊔
Friday	⊔⊔⊔⊔⊔

1. **What was the total number of glasses of water Cliff drank during the 5 days?**

   Ⓐ 27 glasses

   Ⓑ 32 glasses

   Ⓒ 31 glasses

   Ⓓ 28 glasses

2. **How many more glasses did Cliff drink on Thursday than on Monday?**

   Ⓕ 4 glasses

   Ⓖ 8 glasses

   Ⓗ 5 glasses

   Ⓙ 7 glasses

3. **How many glasses of water should Cliff have drunk during the 5 days if he wanted to meet a goal of eight glasses per day?**

   Ⓐ 27 glasses

   Ⓑ 32 glasses

   Ⓒ 31 glasses

   Ⓓ 40 glasses

DIRECTIONS: Choose the best answer.

4. **Giraffes and birds are drinking at a watering hole. There are 10 animals with a total of 30 legs there. How many 2-legged birds are there? How many 4-legged giraffes are there?**

   Ⓕ 5 birds, 5 giraffes

   Ⓖ 4 birds, 3 giraffes

   Ⓗ 2 birds, 5 giraffes

   Ⓙ 6 birds, 1 giraffe

5. **A yard is surrounded by 400 yards of fence. It took Lynne 8 days to paint the whole fence. Which number sentence can Lynne use to figure out how much fence she painted in a day?**

   Ⓐ $400 \times 8 = \blacksquare$

   Ⓑ $400 \div 8 = \blacksquare$

   Ⓒ $400 - 8 = \blacksquare$

   Ⓓ $400 + 8 = \blacksquare$

6. **Five students want to find their average height in inches. Their heights are 54 inches, 56 inches, 52 inches, 57 inches, and 53 inches. How would you find the average height of the students?**

   Ⓕ Add the heights and multiply by 5.

   Ⓖ Add the heights and divide by 5.

   Ⓗ Add the heights and divide by the number of inches in 1 foot.

   Ⓙ Multiply the heights and divide by the number of inches in 1 foot.

STOP

Mathematical Reasoning Standards

2.0 Students use strategies, skills, and concepts in finding solutions:

2.1 Use estimation to verify the reasonableness of calculated results. *(See page 169.)*

2.2 Apply strategies and results from simpler problems to more complex problems. *(See page 170.)*

2.3 Use a variety of methods, such as words, numbers, symbols, charts, graphs, tables, diagrams, and models, to explain mathematical reasoning. *(See page 171.)*

2.4 Express the solution clearly and logically by using the appropriate mathematical notation and terms and clear language; support solutions with evidence in both verbal and symbolic work. *(See page 172.)*

2.5 Indicate the relative advantages of exact and approximate solutions to problems and give answers to a specified degree of accuracy. *(See page 173.)*

What it means:
- Students should understand that sometimes an exact answer is needed (how much change is received on a purchase) and sometimes an estimate is adequate (how much time it takes to get to a friend's house).
- Students should be able to determine how accurate an answer needs to be. If the question asks for the answer to the nearest ten, the student should round the number appropriately.

2.6 Make precise calculations and check the validity of the results from the context of the problem. *(See page 174.)*

3.0 Students move beyond a particular problem by generalizing to other situations:

3.1 Evaluate the reasonableness of the solution in the context of the original situation.

3.2 Note the method of deriving the solution and demonstrate a conceptual understanding of the derivation by solving similar problems.

3.3 Develop generalizations of the results obtained and apply them in other circumstances.

Math

2.1

Using Estimation

DIRECTIONS: Choose the most reasonable answer.

1. **Choose the most reasonable answer. What is the average number of books in a bookstore?**
   - (A) 100
   - (B) 1,000,000
   - (C) 10,000
   - (D) 600

2. **Which equation will have the greatest answer?**
   - (F) $357 - 6 =$
   - (G) $615 - 485 =$
   - (H) $888 - 777 =$
   - (J) $915 - 769 =$

3. **Suppose you are estimating by rounding to the nearest ten. What numbers should you use to estimate if you are rounding numbers between 23 and 46?**
   - (A) 30 and 50
   - (B) 30 and 40
   - (C) 20 and 50
   - (D) 20 and 40

4. **Which of these is the best estimate of**
   $$767 \div 7 = \blacksquare$$
   - (F) 10
   - (G) 11
   - (H) 100
   - (H) 110

5. **Which of these would you probably use to measure a person's waist?**
   - (A) meter stick
   - (B) tape measure
   - (C) yardstick
   - (D) ruler

6. **Which of the following is the closest estimate for the equation?**
   $$358 \times 2 = \blacksquare$$
   - (F) 700
   - (G) 600
   - (H) 900
   - (J) 400

7. **Which number in $1.62 would you look at to round it to the nearest dollar?**
   - (A) 1
   - (B) 6
   - (C) 2
   - (D) None of these

8. **Which number could be put in the circle to make this statement true?**
   $$\frac{8}{7} > \blacksquare$$
   - (F) $\frac{7}{8}$
   - (G) 7
   - (H) 8
   - (J) 8.7

STOP

Math

2.2

Mathematical Reasoning

Solving Problems

DIRECTIONS: Choose the best answer.

1. Which of these numbers is even and a multiple of 12?
   - (A) 34
   - (B) 145
   - (C) 144
   - (D) 148

2. The sum of two numbers is 21 and their product is 98. What are the 2 numbers?
   - (F) 12 and 8
   - (G) 14 and 7
   - (H) 77 and 21
   - (J) 7 and 9

3. There are two numbers whose product is 98 and quotient is 2. What are the two numbers?
   - (A) 49 and 8
   - (B) 14 and 2
   - (C) 14 and 7
   - (D) 96 and 2

4. In this pyramid, each number is the product of the two numbers directly below it. Which number is missing from the pyramid?

   48

   8   ____

   4   2   3

   - (F) 6
   - (G) 4
   - (H) 8
   - (J) None of these

5. How many hundreds are in 100,000?
   - (A) 10
   - (B) 100,000
   - (C) 100
   - (D) 1,000

6. Nicolas has a water bottle that holds 2 gallons. Which of the following would fill it?
   - (F) 4 cups
   - (G) 3 pints
   - (H) 8 quarts
   - (J) 1 liter

7. Larry, Carey, and Harry went out for lunch. Each friend ordered a salad. The choices were egg, tuna, and chicken. Carey won't eat egg. Larry never orders tuna. Harry only likes chicken. Each friend ate something different. Who ordered tuna?
   - (A) Larry
   - (B) Carey
   - (C) Harry
   - (D) Not enough information

8. There were 488 balloons decorating the gymnasium for a party. There were 97 students at the party. If each student brought home an equal number of balloons after the party, how many balloons were left over?
   - (F) 3 balloons
   - (G) 46 balloons
   - (H) 12 balloons
   - (J) None of these

STOP

Solving Problems

DIRECTIONS: Choose the best answer.

1. **You have coins that total $1.23. What coins do you have?**

   (A) 10 dimes, 1 nickel, 3 pennies

   (B) 3 quarter, 3 dimes, 3 pennies

   (C) 4 quarters, 1 dimes, 2 nickels, 3 pennies

   (D) 4 quarters, 3 dimes, 3 pennies

2. **The sum of each column in the number pattern below equals 21. What numbers are missing?**

3	5	2	1	6
2	7	8	9	1
9	8	4	6	7
___	1	7	___	7

   (F) 6 and 8

   (G) 7 and 5

   (H) 1 and 7

   (J) 4 and 3

3. **A shape has 4 sides. Two sides are the same length and one corner is 90 degrees. What is the shape?**

   (A) parallelogram

   (B) rectangle

   (C) triangle

   (D) Not enough information

4. **What coins total $0.71?**

   (F) 3 dimes, 1 nickel, 1 penny

   (G) 1 quarter, 3 dimes, 1 penny

   (H) 2 quarters, 1 dime, 1 nickel

   (J) 2 quarters, 2 dimes, 1 penny

5. **Kim made one straight cut across the trapezoid as shown. Which pair of figures could be the two cut pieces of the trapezoid?**

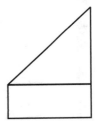

(A)

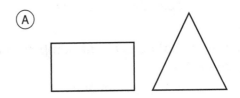

(B)

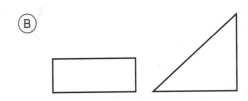

(C)

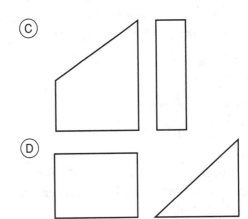

(D)

STOP

Solving Problems

> **Example:**
>
> Look at the problem below. To get the smallest answer, which of these symbols goes in the box ?
>
> 150 ■ 6 =
>
> (A) +
> (B) −
> (C) ×
> (D) ÷
>
> Answer: (D)

DIRECTIONS: Choose the best answer.

1. Which symbol below best completes the equation?

    84.62 ■ 84.26

    (A) >
    (B) =
    (C) <
    (D) None of these

2. Sara wants to measure how much applesauce she made this fall. If she uses metric units, which should she use?

    (F) gram
    (G) liter
    (H) kilogram
    (J) centimeter

3. One tablespoon holds about 15 milliliters. About how many tablespoons of soup are in a 225-milliliter can?

    (A) 45 tablespoons
    (B) 5 tablespoons
    (C) 3,375 tablespoons
    (D) 15 tablespoons

4. How did the temperature change between Saturday and Sunday? On Sunday it was _____.

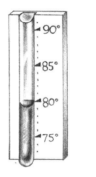

Saturday   **Sunday**

    (F) 5 degrees cooler than Saturday
    (G) 10 degrees cooler than Saturday
    (H) 5 degrees warmer than Saturday
    (J) 10 degrees warmer than Saturday

5. Which of these has the greatest volume?

    (A) 4 quarts
    (B) 2 gallons
    (C) 8 pints
    (D) 17 cups

Math
2.5
Mathematical Reasoning
Exact and Approximate Solutions

 Clue Before you choose an answer, ask yourself, "Does this answer make sense?"

DIRECTIONS: Choose the best answer.

1. **Which of the following would you probably measure in feet?**

   (A) length of a pencil

   (B) distance between two cities

   (C) amount of juice left in a bottle

   (D) the length of a couch

2. **You are mailing in your brother's college application today. It is a regular letter size. You must make sure you have enough postage. How much do you think it weighs?**

   (F) 1 pound

   (G) 8 pounds

   (H) 1 ounce

   (J) 8 ounces

3. **Leslie is making punch in a very large punch bowl. Orange juice comes in different-sized containers. Which size container should she buy in order to purchase the fewest number of containers?**

   (A) a one-cup container

   (B) a one-gallon container

   (C) a one-pint container

   (D) a one-quart container

4. **Trina's family has two dogs. Pepper weighs 31 pounds. Salt weighs 28 pounds. To the nearest ten pounds, how much is the combined weight of the two dogs?**

   (F) 59

   (G) 31

   (H) 28

   (J) 60

5. **Mr. Cook was 25 years old when Mary was born. How old will he be when Mary has her thirteenth birthday?**

   (A) 38

   (B) 12

   (C) 25

   (D) 13

6. **Marcos has $47.82. He plans to spend $25 on presents. How much money will he have left, to the nearest dollar?**

   (F) $22

   (G) $22.82

   (H) $23

   (J) $25

STOP

Math

2.6

Solving Problems

DIRECTIONS: Choose the best answer.

1. There are 62 students on a class trip. They are taking a bus to the nature park. The ride to the park takes 25 minutes and the ride home takes 30 minutes. Lunch at the park costs $3.25 per child. How much does it cost to get into the park?

- (A) $201.50
- (B) $50.00
- (C) $120.25
- (D) Not enough information

2. The school play ran for 3 nights, and 345 people attended each night. Tickets cost $4.25 each. How much money did the school play make?

- (F) $1,239.50
- (G) $1,466.25
- (H) $1,035.00
- (J) $4,398.75

3. Jesse bought a pack of cards for $1.25 and a baseball for $8.39. He has $5.36 left over. With how much money did he start?

- (A) $20.00
- (B) $9.64
- (C) $1.78
- (D) $15.00

4. There are 21 fish in every square yard of water in a lake. If the lake is 812 square yards, how many fish are in the lake?

- (F) 17,052
- (G) 23,708
- (H) 29,987
- (J) 14,879

5. Mona started her chores at 3:30 P.M. She needed to take out the garbage, wash the dishes, water the houseplants, feed the dog, and clean up her room. Mona finished her chores just as her dad came home at 5:20 P.M. How long did it take Mona to do her chores?

- (A) 50 minutes
- (B) 2 hours
- (C) 1 hour, 50 minutes
- (D) None of these

6. If the temperature in the morning is 56°F, what will the temperature be when it rises 25° this afternoon?

- (F) 78°F
- (G) 76°F
- (H) 81°F
- (J) 85°F

7. A chicken pot pie was cut into 8 slices. For dinner, the Wilsons ate $\frac{3}{8}$ of the pie. For lunch, the Wilsons ate $\frac{1}{4}$ of the pie. How much of the pie was eaten in all?

- (A) $\frac{5}{8}$
- (B) $\frac{2}{8}$
- (C) $\frac{4}{12}$
- (D) $\frac{1}{3}$

STOP

Math

2.0

For pages 169–174

| Mini-Test 2 |

Mathematical Reasoning

DIRECTIONS: Choose the best answer.

1. Which of these would you probably use to measure a person's foot length?

   (A) meter stick

   (B) tape measure

   (C) yardstick

   (D) ruler

2. Aidan bought a slice of pizza and a soda at the arcade. The pizza cost $4.50, and the soda cost $2.75. Aidan paid with a ten dollar bill. How much change did he receive?

   (F) $5.50

   (G) $3.00

   (H) $2.75

   (J) $7.25

3. A marching band has 126 members. If only rows of 8 members are formed, how many members are left over?

   (A) 15

   (B) 126

   (C) 8

   (D) 6

4. Which type of graph would be best to show how the average weekly temperature changed in one town from month to month?

   (F) pie chart

   (G) tally chart

   (H) bar graph

   (J) line graph

5. What should replace the ■ in the number sentence below?

   $$7 \ ■ \ 6 = 42$$

   (A) +

   (B) −

   (C) ×

   (D) ÷

6. The Empire State Building is 1,472 feet tall. Mount Everest is 20 times taller than that. How tall is Mount Everest?

   (F) 1,472 + 20

   (G) 1,472 × 20

   (H) 1,472 ÷ 20

   (J) 1,472 − 20

7. Each day 7,500 tons of ore can be processed. How many tons of ore can be processed in 25 days?

   (A) 188

   (B) 187,500

   (C) 188,000

   (D) 8

8. 7 pirates want to share 1,006 coins so that each will get the same number of coins. How many coins will be left over?

   (F) 5

   (G) 7

   (H) 143

   (J) 1,001

STOP

175

How Am I Doing?

Mini-Test 1 Page 167 **Number Correct**	**6** answers correct	**Great Job!** Move on to the section test on page 177.
	4–5 answers correct	**You're almost there!** But you still need a little practice. Review practice pages 165–166 before moving on to the section test on page 177.
	0–3 answers correct	**Oops!** Time to review what you have learned and try again. Review the practice section on pages 165–166. Then retake the test on page 167. Now move on to the section test on page 177.
Mini-Test 2 Page 175 **Number Correct**	**7–8** answers correct	**Awesome!** Move on to the section test on page 177.
	5–6 answers correct	**You're almost there!** But you still need a little practice. Review practice pages 169–174 before moving on to the section test on page 177.
	0–4 answers correct	**Oops!** Time to review what you have learned and try again. Review the practice section on pages 169–174. Then retake the test on page 175. Now move on to the section test on page 177.

Name _____   Date _____

Final Mathematical Reasoning Test
for pages 164–175

DIRECTIONS: The graph shows how many students participated in a school olympics program. Use the graph for numbers 1–3.

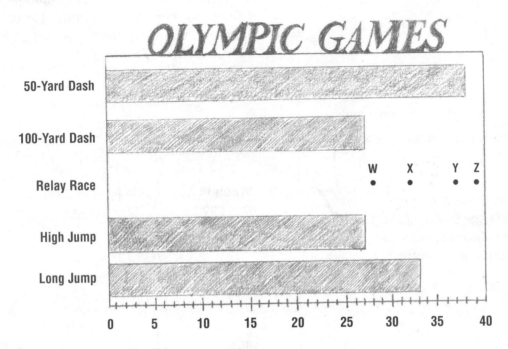

1. After this graph was made, 4 students switched from the 50-yard dash to the high jump. How many students then competed in the high jump?

   Ⓐ 29
   Ⓑ 30
   Ⓒ 31
   Ⓓ 33

2. The graph is not complete. There are 28 students who competed in the relay race. Which point should the bar be drawn to?

   Ⓕ Point W
   Ⓖ Point X
   Ⓗ Point Y
   Ⓙ Point Z

3. When the graph was made, which event was the most popular?

   Ⓐ 50-yard dash
   Ⓑ 100-yard dash
   Ⓒ high jump
   Ⓓ long jump

GO

DIRECTIONS: Choose the best answer.

4. Jodi bought cans of tennis balls that cost $2.50 per can. What else do you need to know to find out how much money Jodi spent in all?

(F) whether she played singles or doubles

(G) how many cans of tennis balls she bought

(H) whether she won her tennis match

(J) how many cans of tennis balls the store had in stock

5. Ellie saved her allowance to buy a new pair of sneakers for $62.35. She had $70.00. After buying the sneakers, how much money did she have left?

(A) $9.25

(B) $8.75

(C) $7.65

(D) $6.75

6. Gerald's desk has 5 pencils, 3 erasers, and 2 boxes of crayons. There are 16 crayons in each box. How many crayons does Gerald have?

(F) 30

(G) 10

(H) 26

(J) 32

7. Al counted 156 red leaves on his tree. Three days later, he counted 94 leaves. How many leaves fell off the tree during those three days?

(A) 282

(B) 62

(C) 156

(D) 253

8. Noriko was looking at a map of Glacier National Park. He noted the heights of five mountain peaks: Rockwell at 9,272 feet; Going-to-the-Sun at 9,642 feet; Thunderbird at 8,520 feet; Kaina at 9,489 feet; and Cleveland at 10,466 feet. If the mountains were arranged in order of height, which mountain would be in the middle?

(F) Kaina

(G) Going-to-the-Sun

(H) Thunderbird

(J) Rockwell

9. Which is the best way to estimate 47 ×53?

(A) 50 × 60

(B) 40 × 60

(C) 50 × 50

(D) 40 × 50

10. Which is the best way to estimate $83\overline{)26}$?

(F) $85\overline{)25}$

(G) $80\overline{)25}$

(H) $80\overline{)30}$

(J) $90\overline{)20}$

11. Toby left his house for school at 7:35 A.M. He arrived at school at 7:50 A.M., which was 10 minutes before school started. How long before school started did Toby leave the house?

(A) 10 minutes

(B) 15 minutes

(C) 25 minutes

(D) not enough information

GO

12. Which of the following is the closest estimate for the equation 254 ÷ 2?

- (F) 100
- (G) 125
- (H) 500
- (J) 300

13. Which of the following is the closest estimate for the equation 594 ÷ 31?

- (A) 600
- (B) 30
- (C) 35
- (D) 20

14. What is the value of 1 nickel, 2 dimes, 1 quarter, and 1 penny?

- (F) $0.56
- (G) $0.50
- (H) $0.51
- (J) $0.57

15. If Jerry walked 2 miles for charity, how many feet did he walk?

- (A) 20 feet
- (B) 6 feet
- (C) 3,520 feet
- (D) 10,560 feet

16. David scored 1,832 points on a video game. Susan scored 2 times more than David. Paul scored 234 points less than Susan. What was Paul's score?

- (F) 3,320 points
- (G) 3,664 points
- (H) 3,430 points
- (J) 468 points

17. Each side of a square is an odd number of inches. The total length of its sides will be _____.

- (A) an even number
- (B) an odd number
- (C) always greater than 40 inches
- (D) either an even or an odd number

18. When you subtract 5 from a number larger than 10, the answer will be _____.

- (F) odd or even
- (G) always less than 10
- (H) always even
- (J) always odd

19. Use the number 580. If you add to it any number that has a 4 in the tens place, what must be in the answer?

- (A) four ones
- (B) two tens
- (C) five hundreds
- (D) four tens

20. The sides of an equilateral triangle are all the same length. If each side is an odd number in length, then the total length of its sides will be _____.

- (F) less than the length of one side
- (G) an odd number
- (H) an even number
- (J) either an even or an odd number

GO

21. A circus has 13 elephants. Twinkle weighs 8,100 pounds. Peanut weighs 11,423 pounds. Which number sentence will tell how much more Peanut weighs than Twinkle?

   - (A) 8,100 − 11,423
   - (B) 11,423 − 8,100
   - (C) 11,423 + 8,100
   - (D) 13 × 8,100

22. Six musicians gave a concert. There were 273 people in the audience. Nine people left early. Fifteen people were sitting in the front row. Which number sentence shows how many people were in the audience until the end?

   - (F) 9 × 15
   - (G) 273 + 9 + 15
   - (H) 273 + 9
   - (J) 273 − 9

23. Choose the operation sign that makes 3 ▧ 4 =12 true.

   - (A) +
   - (B) −
   - (C) ×
   - (D) ÷

24. Choose the operation sign that makes 15 ▧ 5 =3 true.

   - (F) +
   - (G) −
   - (H) ×
   - (J) ÷

25. An auto dealer hopes to sell twice as many cars this year as last year. He sold 1,056 cars last year. To the nearest hundred, how many cars does the dealer hope to sell this year?

   - (A) 2,100
   - (B) 2,000
   - (C) 1,100
   - (D) 500

26. The supermarket sells an average of 1,028 dozen eggs each week. To the nearest thousand, how many eggs will be sold in 6 weeks?

   - (F) 6,000
   - (G) 200
   - (H) 74,000
   - (J) 12,000

27. A tank contains 555 liters of oil. Nine liters of oil are used each day. Approximately how many days will the supply last?

   - (A) 58
   - (B) 60
   - (C) 62
   - (D) 64

28. In one hour, 560 loaves of bread can be baked. How many loaves can be baked in 112 hours, to the nearest hundred?

   - (F) 62,700
   - (G) 63,000
   - (H) 62,000
   - (J) 600

STOP

Name _____   Date _____

Mathematical Reasoning Test
Answer Sheet

1 Ⓐ Ⓑ Ⓒ Ⓓ
2 Ⓕ Ⓖ Ⓗ Ⓙ
3 Ⓐ Ⓑ Ⓒ Ⓓ
4 Ⓕ Ⓖ Ⓗ Ⓙ
5 Ⓐ Ⓑ Ⓒ Ⓓ
6 Ⓕ Ⓖ Ⓗ Ⓙ
7 Ⓐ Ⓑ Ⓒ Ⓓ
8 Ⓕ Ⓖ Ⓗ Ⓙ
9 Ⓐ Ⓑ Ⓒ Ⓓ
10 Ⓕ Ⓖ Ⓗ Ⓙ

11 Ⓐ Ⓑ Ⓒ Ⓓ
12 Ⓕ Ⓖ Ⓗ Ⓙ
13 Ⓐ Ⓑ Ⓒ Ⓓ
14 Ⓕ Ⓖ Ⓗ Ⓙ
15 Ⓐ Ⓑ Ⓒ Ⓓ
16 Ⓕ Ⓖ Ⓗ Ⓙ
17 Ⓐ Ⓑ Ⓒ Ⓓ
18 Ⓕ Ⓖ Ⓗ Ⓙ
19 Ⓐ Ⓑ Ⓒ Ⓓ
20 Ⓕ Ⓖ Ⓗ Ⓙ

21 Ⓐ Ⓑ Ⓒ Ⓓ
22 Ⓕ Ⓖ Ⓗ Ⓙ
23 Ⓐ Ⓑ Ⓒ Ⓓ
24 Ⓕ Ⓖ Ⓗ Ⓙ
25 Ⓐ Ⓑ Ⓒ Ⓓ
26 Ⓕ Ⓖ Ⓗ Ⓙ
27 Ⓐ Ⓑ Ⓒ Ⓓ
28 Ⓕ Ⓖ Ⓗ Ⓙ

Answer Key

Page 8
1. D
2. F
3. A
4. H
5. G
6. B
7. C
8. E

Page 9
1. B
2. H
3. B
4. G
5. C
6. F
7. D
8. H

Page 10
1. A
2. H
3. B
4. F
5. C
6. H
7. D
8. G

Page 11
1. D
2. H
3. A
4. H
5. D
6. H
7. H

Page 12
1. D
2. G
3. D
4. F
5. C
6. J
7. D

Page 13 Mini-Test
1. B
2. F
3. B
4. G
5. B
6. J
7. B
8. F
9. C

Page 15
1. B
2. F
3. D
4. F

Page 16
1. D
2. F
3. B
4. a. The sun causes water to evaporate from Earth.
   b. Clouds form when the water in the air cools.
   c. Fog is a low cloud.

Page 17
1. B
2. G
3. B

Page 18
1. D
2. H
3. A

Page 19
1. The people of Rabaul had an escape plan. They knew the volcano had erupted before and prepared for the next time.
2. Scientists told them to leave when they noticed earthquakes.
3. Make an escape plan. If the volcano begins to smoke or there is an earthquake in the area, begin the escape plan.

Page 20
1. B
2. J
3. T
   F
   T
   F

Page 21
1. B
2. F
3. D
4. G

Page 22 Mini-Test
1. B
2. H
3. C

Page 24
1. D
2. The story is about an animal and has a moral.
3. A fable is usually about animals. A fable includes details about a moral or character lesson.

Page 25
1. D
2. G
3. A
4. H

Page 26
1. B
2. H
3. C
4. F

Page 27
1. why the sun and moon appear in the sky
2. why porcupines have four claws on each foot
3. One Who Walks All Over the Sky and Walking About Early; Porcupine and Beaver
4. They both cared abut and wanted to change their environment

Page 28

1. ice
2. a snowstorm
3. kite
4. the night
5. mice
   Answers will vary for numbers 6–10. Examples include:
6. a lunch as cold as ice
7. a friend like a sister
8. a coat as warm as a soft blanket
9. a winter day like a beautiful painting
10. with a smile that sparkled like sunshine

Page 29 Mini-Test

1. C
2. F
3. After they started going so fast down the hill; twist, a loop, fast turns, everyone screamed in delight

Page 31 Final Reading Test

1. C
2. F
3. C
4. F
5. A
6. H
7. A
8. H
9. A
10. G
11. C
12. J
13. D
14. F
15. B
16. J
17. D
18. J
19. D
20. F
21. C
22. J
23. B
24. G
25. B
26. J
27. C
28. F
29. C
30. G
31. A
32. G
33. B
34. G
35. A
36. F

Page 37

Land Mammals: people, elephants, rabbits, dogs, cats
Both: seal, walrus, otter
Water Mammals: dolphins, whales

Page 38

1. hide, bone, and fish
2. B
3. Glue is used to **stick things together**. Glues are made of **gelatin, which comes from boiling animal parts and bones**. Long ago, ancient people used **sticky juices from plants and insects** for making paint. Today, there are **many special** kinds of glue.

Page 39

1. C
2. F
3. Answers will vary but students should indicate that an outline helps to organize details in a logical order.

Page 40

1. Earth revolves around the sun while spinning on its axis. The Earth is tilted on its axis and moves in an oval, rather than a circle, around the sun.
2. The information came from the book *All About Earth*.
3. Students should writer their answers for a kindergarten-level reader. Example: The Earth spins around. But it is not straight up and down as it spins—it leans. When it leans toward the sun, we have summer. When it leans away from the sun, we have winter.
4. C

Page 41

1. D
2. H
3. D
4. G

Page 42

1. C
2. H
3. D
4. G
5. C
6. J

Page 43
1. A
2. H
3. D
4. G

Page 44
1. A
2. G
3. D
4. J

Page 45 Mini-Test
1. A
2. G
3. B
4. J
5. B
6. J
7. C
8. G

Page 47
1. Hannah's family car has broken down in the middle of the desert.
2. Answers will vary but students should give two possible endings to the story.
3. Answers will vary but students should list sights, sounds, and feelings that someone would experience in this situation. Example: very little sound, miles and miles of sand, and perhaps fear.
4. Students should write an ending to this story.

Page 48
1. Answers will vary. The narrator likes the family tradition but some students might say that the narrator hints that he or she might like more presents of her own.
2. Maggie hugged her stuffed animal and looked at the narrator.
3. Because it is not like a traditional birthday.
4. Yes, because she seems to enjoy the happiness the tradition brings to others.

Page 49
1. The main idea is how bats use echolocation to navigate.
2. Defining each word helps to clearly explain how echolocation works.
3. Answers will vary. Examples: more about animals that use echolocation or more about how echolocation works
4. encyclopedia, books about bats, Internet

Page 50
1. Samuel Morse's invention of the telegraph.
2. Students should list three details that helped them to determine the main idea of the passage.
3. Students should write a brief summary of the passage.

Page 51 Mini-Test
1. C
2. G
3. A
4. J

Page 53 Final Writing Test
1. C
2. F
3. D
4. F
5. C
6. G
7. D
8. H
9. C
10. H
11. B
12. F
13. B
14. H
15. D
16. F
17. D
18. J
19. C
20. F
21. B

Page 60
1. B
2. J
3. B
4. Yes, I will go to the library with you.
5. No, I don't know of any books about swamp monsters.
6. Yes, I'm sure the library's computer will help you.
7. Well, how do you use the library's computer?
8. Well, you can start by following the directions on the computer's screen.
9. Yes, the librarian will help you if you need it.

Page 61
1. C
2. J
3. B
4. G
5. C
6. H

Page 62
1. B
2. J
3. D
4. G
5. D
6. G
7. B
8. F
9. A

Page 63
1. B
2. F
3. C
4. does not
5. could not
6. were not
7. must not
8. did not
9. H
10. B
11. G

Page 64
1. A
2. H
3. B
4. J
5. A

Page 65
1. Tyson began singing "The Star-Spangled Banner."
2. Joe read an article about Canada geese in a magazine called *Migrating Birds*. (underlined)
3. We sold school supplies to help raise money for the Red Cross.
4. Abby said, "Yes, I'm really glad you are here."
5. D
6. F
7. A
8. G

Page 66
1. C
2. F
3. B
4. J
5. C
6. H
7. D
8. J
9. A

Page 67 Mini-Test
1. Horses can walk, trot, and gallop.
2. The thoroughbred, standardbred, and quarter horse are used for pleasure riding.
3. B
4. J
5. C
6. H
7. B
8. F
9. B

Page 69 Final Language Conventions Test
1. B
2. J
3. A
4. G
5. B
6. G
7. A
8. J
9. C
10. F
11. B
12. G
13. B
14. H
15. D
16. G
17. C
18. F
19. C
20. F
21. B
22. J
23. D
24. F
25. B
26. F
27. A
28. J
29. D
30. H
31. B
32. F
33. B
34. F
35. D
36. J
37. C
38. G
39. C

Page 76
1. D
2. F
3. A
4. J
5. B
6. H
7. D

Page 77
1. D
2. F
3. B
4. F
5. B
6. G
7. C
8. H
9. C

Page 78
1. A
2. F
3. C
4. J
5. C
6. H
7. A
8. H

Page 79
1. Jose's mother should estimate the costs, add the tax, and round the number up. It's better to have too much money than not enough.
2. The clerk knows the prices and tax, so the amount will be exact.
3. To order carpet, Mr. Mason will need to know exactly how big the space is.
4. If you subtract the number on the odometer before the trip from the number after the trip, the answer will be exact.
5. The amount will vary because it is not measured exactly as it is poured from the bottle.
6. The amount of time will be an estimate because speed and conditions could vary.
7. The temperature will be an exact measure because of the use of a thermometer.
8. They should estimate how many pictures they want to take and buy enough to cover that rounded amount.
9. Rashawn has to buy the exact number of tickets because each person will need one.

Page 80
1. C
2. J
3. A
4. H

Page 81
1. B
2. D
3. E
4. C
5. A
6. A
7. H
8. A
9. H
10. D
11. F
12. A

Page 82
1. D
2. F
3. C
4. F
5. D
6. G

Page 83
1. D
2. F
3. D
4. H
5. A
6. F
7. B
8. J

Page 84
1. D
2. F
3. D
4. H
5. B
6. F
7. C
8. H

Page 85 Mini-Test
1. 2,3,4,1
2. 220 mph; 62,000 pieces; 300,000 pounds
3. $\frac{71}{100}$; 0.71
4. right
5. A
6. H
7. B
8. J

Page 87
1. D
2. F
3. C
4. J
5. A
6. F
7. C
8. G

Page 88
1. B
2. J
3. A
4. H
5. B
6. H
7. A
8. G
9. D
10. F

Page 89 Mini-Test
1. C
2. J
3. A
4. J
5. B
6. F
7. B
8. 0.5
9. 0.9
10. 0
11. 6
12. 19

Page 91
1. B
2. H
3. A
4. G
5. C
6. J
7. A
8. H
9. B
10. G

Page 92
1. D
2. F
3. D
4. F
5. C
6. G
7. C
8. J
9. A
10. H

Page 93
1. C
2. F
3. G
4. A
5. J
6. D
7. F
8. G

Page 94
1. C
2. J
3. D
4. G
5. A
6. J
7. D
8. F

Page 95 Mini-Test
1. A
2. H
3. C
4. J
5. A
6. J
7. C
8. F

Page 97
1. B
2. G
3. D
4. F
5. A
6. G
7. D
8. G
9. B

Page 98
1. C
2. H
3. C
4. G
5. A
6. F
7. D
8. G

Page 99 Mini-Test
1. A
2. J
3. C
4. G
5. A
6. H
7. C
8. H
9. B
10. H

Page 102 Final Number Sense Test
1. C
2. F
3. B
4. J
5. A
6. H
7. D
8. F
9. B
10. G
11. D
12. F
13. A
14. H
15. C
16. F
17. D
18. G
19. D
20. F
21. B
22. H
23. C
24. H
25. A
26. G
27. A
28. H
29. C
30. J
31. A
32. H
33. C
34. G
35. B

Page 108
1. B
2. H
3. D
4. H
5. A
6. G
7. B
8. J
9. D
10. H

Page 109
1. B
2. G
3. C
4. G
5. A
6. J
7. A
8. G
9. A
10. G

Page 110
1. B
2. F
3. C
4. J
5. B
6. J
7. A
8. H

Page 111
1. A
2. G
3. D
4. F
5. C
6. H
7. C

Page 112
1. C
2. F
3. D
4. G
5. C
6. F
7. D
8. H

Page 113 Mini-Test
1. D
2. H
3. B
4. G
5. B
6. J
7. B
8. F

Page 115
1. D
2. F
3. C
4. J
5. C
6. F
7. B
8. H
9. C

Page 116
1. A
2. G
3. C
4. F
5. D
6. G
7. A
8. H

Page 117 Mini-Test
1. B
2. J
3. A
4. G
5. D
6. H
7. C
8. H
9. C

Page 119 Final Algebra and Functions Test
1. B
2. H
3. B
4. J
5. A
6. H
7. B
8. F
9. D
10. H
11. C
12. F
13. C
14. H
15. D
16. G
17. A
18. H
19. D
20. H
21. A
22. F
23. C
24. F
25. D
26. H
27. A
28. G
29. A
30. J
31. D
32. J
33. A
34. G
35. D
36. F
37. A
38. J
39. B
40. F
41. B
42. H

Page 125
1. D
2. F
3. C
4. G
5. B
6. G
7. C

Page 126
1. B
2. H
3. D
4. F
5. C
6. G
7. A
8. J

Page 127
1. C
2. F
3. D
4. G
5. B
6. J
7. A
8. J

Page 128
1. C
2. J
3. A
4. G
5. A
6. G
7. A
8. H

Page 129 Mini-Test
1. C
2. F
3. A
4. G
5. A
6. J
7. B
8. F
9. C

Page 131
1. Graphs should show coordinates that satisfy the equation $y = 3x + 1$. Example: (0,1) (1,4)(2,7)(3,10)
2. Graphs should show coordinates that satisfy the equation $y = 2x - 1$. Example: (1,1) (2,3)(3,5)(4,7)
3. Graphs should show coordinates that satisfy the equation $y = x + 1$. Example: (1,2) (2,3)(3,4)(4,5)
4. Graphs should show coordinates that satisfy the equation $y = 2x$. Example: (1,2) (2,4)(3,6)(4,8)

Page 132
1. C
2. J
3. C
4. G
5. D
6. G

Page 133
1. A
2. G
3. D
4. G
5. D
6. G

Page 134 Mini-Test
1. Graphs should show coordinates that satisfy the equation $y = x + 3$. Example: (1,4) (2,5)(3,6)(4,7)
2. Graphs should show coordinates that satisfy the equation $y = x - 1$. Example: (2,1) (3,2)(4,3)(5,4)
3. A
4. G
5. A
6. F

Page 136
1. B
2. H
3. D
4. J
5. A
6. J
7. B
8. H
9. D

Page 137
1. B
2. H
3. D
4. H
5. B
6. H
7. D
8. H

Page 138
1. D
2. H
3. D
4. J

Page 139
1. C
2. J
3. C
4. G

Page 140
1. C
2. G
3. A
4. J
5. B
6. F
7. D
8. H

Page 141
1. A
2. J
3. C
4. G
5. C
6. G

Page 142
1. B
2. F
3. C
4. G
5. A
6. J
7. C
8. F

Page 143
1. C
2. G
3. A
4. J
5. D
6. G
7. A

Page 144 Mini-Test
1. A
2. H
3. C
4. F
5. B
6. H
7. B
8. J
9. A

Page 146 Final Measurement and Geometry Test
1. B
2. J
3. C
4. G
5. D
6. F
7. D
8. H
9. A
10. J
11. B
12. J
13. B
14. H
15. B
16. J
17. C
18. G
19. A
20. H
21. C
22. J
23. A
24. F
25. B
26. J
27. C
28. H
29. A
30. J

Page 152
1. B
2. F
3. D
4. J
5. D
6. H

Page 153
1. B
2. H
3. A
4. G
5. A
6. J
7. D
8. H

Page 154
1. C
2. F
3. A
4. F
5. D
6. G

Page 155 Mini-Test
1. C
2. J
3. C
4. H
5. D
6. G

Page 157
1. B
2. J
3. A
4. F
5. C
6. J

Page 158
1. D
2. F
3. C
4. G
5. A
6. F

Page 159 Mini-Test
1. C
2. G
3. D
4. G
5. A
6. J

Page 161 Final Statistics, Data Analysis, and Probability Test
1. A
2. F
3. A
4. G
5. D
6. H
7. A
8. J
9. D
10. F
11. C
12. G
13. B
14. H

Page 165
1. C
2. G
3. C
4. J
5. B

Page 166
1. C
2. F
3. C
4. G
5. D
6. H
7. D

Page 167 Mini-Test
1. B
2. F
3. D
4. F
5. B
6. G

Page 169
1. C
2. F
3. C
4. H
5. B
6. F
7. B
8. F

Page 170
1. C
2. G
3. C
4. F
5. D
6. H
7. B
8. F

Page 171
1. C
2. G
3. D
4. J
5. B

Page 172
1. A
2. G
3. D
4. H
5. B

Page 173
1. D
2. J
3. B
4. J
5. A
6. H

Page 174
1. D
2. J
3. D
4. F
5. C
6. H
7. A

Page 175
1. D
2. H
3. D
4. H
5. C
6. G
7. B
8. F

Page 177 Final Mathematical Reasoning Test
1. C
2. F
3. A
4. G
5. C
6. J
7. B
8. F
9. C
10. H
11. C
12. G
13. D
14. H
15. D
16. H
17. A
18. F
19. B
20. G
21. B
22. J
23. C
24. J
25. A
26. H
27. C
28. F